DESIGNING FOR WINDOWS 8

Brent Schooley

Apress·

President and Publisher: Paul Manning
Lead Editor: Gwenan Spearing
Technical Reviewer: Alejandro Toledo
Editorial Board: Steve Anglin, Mark Beckner, Ewan Buckingham, Gary Cornell,
    Louise Corrigan, Morgan Ertel, Jonathan Gennick, Jonathan Hassell,
    Robert Hutchinson, Michelle Lowman, James Markham, Matthew Moodie,
    Jeff Olson, Jeffrey Pepper, Douglas Pundick, Ben Renow-Clarke, Dominic Shakeshaft,
    Gwenan Spearing, Matt Wade, Tom Welsh
Coordinating Editor: Christine Ricketts
Copy Editor: Michael G. Laraque
Compositor: SPi Global
Indexer: SPi Global
Artist: SPi Global
Cover Designer: Anna Ishchenko

Distributed to the book trade worldwide by Springer Science+Business Media New York, 233 Spring Street, 6th Floor, New York, NY 10013. Phone 1-800-SPRINGER, fax (201) 348-4505, e-mail orders-ny@springer-sbm.com, or visit www.springeronline.com. Apress Media, LLC is a California LLC and the sole member (owner) is Springer Science+Business Media Finance Inc (SSBM Finance Inc). SSBM Finance Inc is a **Delaware** corporation.

For information on translations, please e-mail rights@apress.com, or visit www.apress.com.

Apress and friends of ED books may be purchased in bulk for academic, corporate, or promotional use. eBook versions and licenses are also available for most titles. For more information, reference our Special Bulk Sales–eBook Licensing web page at www.apress.com/bulk-sales.

Any source code or other supplementary materials referenced by the author in this text is available to readers at www.apress.com For detailed information about how to locate your book's source code, go to www.apress.com/source-code/

To my parents, who always made me believe anything is possible

Contents

About the Author vii

About the Technical Reviewer ix

Acknowledgments xi

Introduction xiii

Chapter 1:   Microsoft Design Style Inspirations 1

Chapter 2:   Microsoft Design Style Principles 13

Chapter 3:   Design Strategies for Windows 8 39

Chapter 4:   Basic Building Blocks of Windows 8 Design 71

Chapter 5:   Windows 8 Platform Considerations 109

Chapter 6:   Bringing Existing Apps to Windows 8 133

Index 149

About the Author

Brent Schooley is a Technical Evangelist for Infragistics with a focus on mobile platforms. He has been working with Microsoft technologies since 2004. His interests include client- and mobile-application development and user-experience design, with a recent emphasis on Windows 8 and Windows Phone. With keen attention to detail and strong technical and design crossover skills, Brent has always been able to relate to both designers and developers to help them achieve their goals.

About the Technical Reviewer

Alejandro Toledo is an Experience Program Manager and Developer. He recently cofounded a boutique design studio with his brother Arturo, providing experience architecture, user-interface design, and design-education services. Alejandro is also a polyglot involved in an ongoing study of multiple languages spoken around the world. Possessed of an inquisitive mind, Alejandro enjoys spending time with designers and developers, helping them to produce the best possible apps for Windows and Windows Phone. He draws inspiration and energy from his wife and young daughter.

Acknowledgments

First and foremost, I must thank my colleagues at Infragistics for the guidance and support they have provided throughout this process. In particular, many thanks go to Ambrose Little and George Abraham for helping to shape the original presentation content that inspired this book. This book also wouldn't have been possible without my fantastic boss, Jason Beres, allowing me some time during the workweek to dedicate to the book. I also want to thank my CEO, Dean Guida, for fostering an environment where creativity can truly shine. Thank you also to Nick Landry, Dara Monasch, and Bill Hazard for providing much needed support throughout this process.

I also want to acknowledge the various attendees of user groups, code camps, and conferences where I presented my "Designing for Windows 8" session. The questions asked and comments made during these sessions helped shape the material in this book. The energy and enthusiasm all of you showed for this topic helped keep me motivated to complete this book.

Many thanks go to my wonderful family—everyone from my parents and grandparents to aunts, uncles, and cousins. All of you have been very supportive, and I couldn't have finished this without that support!

Finally, I want to thank my wonderful editorial staff at Apress. Big thanks go to Gwenan Spearing for seeking me out as a writer for this topic. This is my first book, and Gwenan had faith in my ability to write about this subject. Christine Ricketts has done a fantastic job of helping me through the editorial process. Ben Renow-Clarke's help in focusing and restructuring the early portions of the book made the end product much more approachable and understandable than I had originally envisioned. Everyone involved in the process has been very understanding concerning the various delays encountered. Thank you for your faith in me and for helping me reach the finish line.

Introduction

Windows 8 offers exciting new opportunities for developers and designers. Microsoft has created a platform for touch-first applications that features a clean design language inspired by major design movements. This marks the first time that design is paramount in creating Windows applications. This can be a challenge for Windows developers who may not have had to concern themselves with design before. If you are going to build Windows Store applications, you will have to understand the fundamentals of designing for the platform. Designing for Windows 8 has been written to help both developers and designers understand what is necessary to create well-designed applications for Windows 8.

The book is divided roughly into two parts. The first three chapters introduce design fundamentals and strategies. Chapter 1 provides some insight into the design inspirations that helped shape the design language used in Windows Store application development. Chapter 2 introduces the design principles that will help guide your design process. Chapter 3 provides some design strategies that will help you keep your design focused. The final three chapters provide practical information on how to design your application. Chapter 4 introduces the basic building blocks of Windows Store applications and discusses some styling tips for each. Chapter 5 provides information specific to the Windows 8 platform that you need to keep in mind as you build your application. Chapter 6 brings everything together and shows how to bring applications from other platforms to Windows 8.

The reference application for this book, Running Total, is available from http://bit.ly/runningtotal. This post describes how to get the application up and running and walks through how the application works. The app is still evolving, so I have also created a GitHub project for the application at https://github.com/brentschooley/Running-Total. Both options for getting Running Total include a beta of Infragistics NetAdvantage for Windows UI controls.

Microsoft Design Style Inspirations

In order to truly understand something, it is often important to understand where it originated. This is especially true of design-related topics. Almost everything designed today has roots somewhere in the past. The Microsoft Design Style is no exception. There are three major design influences that contributed to the formation of this design language: Bauhaus (and the related Modern Design Movement), International Typographic Style (also known as Swiss Design Style), and cinematography (and the related discipline motion design). Each of these had an impact on the creation of the design language that has been used in products such as Zune, Xbox 360, Windows Phone, and now Windows 8.

In this chapter, I'll briefly introduce the three major design influences on Windows 8 design style and the Windows 8 design concepts that were based on these influences. This knowledge is the foundation you'll need to understand why certain decisions were made in Windows 8 application design and why they are so vital to the design of your application. Also, to make sure it is perfectly clear why these points are so important, I will offer you an example for each one, using the sample application "Running Total." In Chapter 2, I will tie these concepts to the Microsoft Design Style Principles that are critical to the success of your Windows 8 application design.

Bauhaus and the Modern Design Movement

The late 1910s were years of great artistic exploration and experimentation. Many designs of the time began to favor form over function. Designs that favor form over function feature heavy adornment and contortion of shapes for solely decorative purposes. The founder of the Bauhaus movement, Walter Gropius, had different views about design:

> Our guiding principle was that design is neither an intellectual nor a material affair, but simply an integral part of the stuff of life, necessary for everyone in a civilized society.

The key piece of this statement is the part stating "design is neither an intellectual nor a material affair, but simply an integral part of the stuff of life." In essence, what Gropius is saying is that we should not be thinking really hard about how to embellish our designs. It is much more important to allow our designs to represent their content authentically and true to their intended function. Another quote from Gropius that further drives this point home is the following regarding the architecture of the time:

> A modern building should derive its architectural significance solely from the vigor and consequence of its own organic proportions. It must be true to itself, logically transparent, and virginal of lies or trivialities.

Though this quote is about architecture, it is just as applicable to our topic if "modern software" is substituted for "modern building." Modern designs should be true to themselves. They also shouldn't be embellished with extraneous things that don't really help explain the concept they intend to convey.

Applying Bauhaus to Running Total

What does this mean for your Windows 8 app? The concepts of the Bauhaus design movement are the guiding force behind a design guidance called *content before chrome*. I will discuss this concept in more detail in Chapter 3, but for now you can think of it as removing all of the buttons and tabs and navigation trees and other application chrome we have in traditional applications. If we strip away all of the chrome that normally gets in the way of our software designs, we can really begin to let the content of our applications shine.

Let's take a look at how these concepts are applied in our Running Total application (see Figure 1-1). One thing you should notice right away is that there is no traditional application menu (File, Edit, etc.). There also are no buttons or tabs on the surface of the application. The top level of runs is grouped by month, but instead of there being a list of months to select, the runs are laid out visually. The group header for the month is a fully interactive piece of content that not only provides the total number of runs for the month but also can be tapped to navigate to that month. Functionality for filtering runs is tucked away in the app bar at the bottom of the screen. Sharing and Settings functionality that might usually accompany the content have a convenient and consistent location within the Windows 8 Charms bar (more on this in Chapter 2).

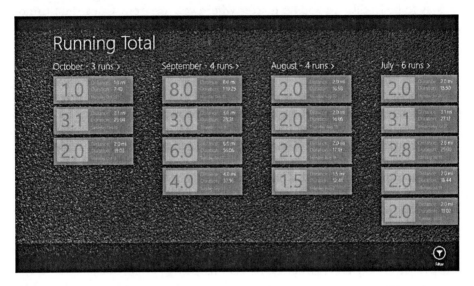

Figure 1-1. Screenshot of Running Total main screen with app bar showing Filter

The good news about all of this is that you don't need to focus on creating and designing tabs and buttons and other navigational chrome in Windows 8. You can simply focus on presenting your content without other stuff getting in the way. This will save you some time, and the end result is an application that lets your content shine.

International Typographic Style (Swiss Design Style)

Another key influence on the design style used for Windows 8 applications is what is known as either International Typographic Style or Swiss Design Style. International Typographic Style focuses on a few key concepts: alignment to a typographic grid, clean and consistent typography, clear iconography, use of photographic imagery, and bold use of colors. Because this is probably the most important influence on Windows 8 application design, I will explain each of the related concepts in its own section.

However, before I address each of these concepts in detail, it bears mentioning that you probably see this design style every day without realizing it. It is called the International Typographic Style because it is used on road signs, subway and train signs, airport signage, and signs leading to such things as bathrooms and stairways in various buildings around the world. Whether you are in New York City or Paris, the signs you see in public areas are designed in such a way as to be familiar to you no matter where you are from. Consistent use of colors and icons helps to guide you to where you need to go.

Typographic Grids

A typographic grid is a system of horizontal and vertical lines that defines the structure of a design. A typographic grid allows for content to be aligned in a consistent manner that usually results in an easy-to-follow organization and information hierarchy. The grid defines sections within the design area, also known as the format, in which elements can be placed and how these elements should be aligned. The simplest grids consist of rows and columns, but some sophisticated grids may define diagonal grid sections as well. A grid is a guideline that should be adhered to but can be broken occasionally for emphasis.

Applying a Typographic Grid to Running Total

The typographic grid for Windows 8 is one of the most rigid and consistent design guidelines in Windows 8. Figures 1-2, 1-3, and 1-4 present screenshots of Windows 8 apps, including Windows Store and Running Total, with some of the major gridlines overlaid above them.

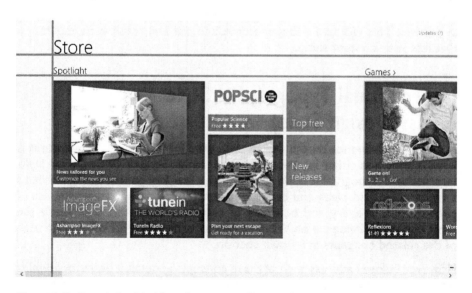

Figure 1-2. *Store hub with title and content gridline overlays*

Figure 1-3. Store section details with title and content gridline overlays

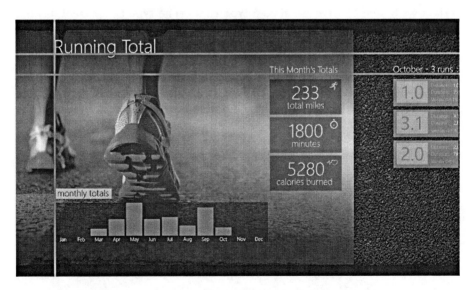

Figure 1-4. Running Total with title and content gridline overlays

Notice how the left edge of the title in each of the screenshots is in the exact same location, 120 pixels from the left side of the screen. The baseline of the same title is exactly 100 pixels below the top of the screen. The content region starts 140 pixels below the top of the screen at the same 120 pixels from the left as the title. Why does this matter? This prescribed placement and alignment of key areas of the screen leads to a consistent experience across Windows 8 applications. Your application needs to conform to these guidelines, or it will stick out like a sore thumb. Thankfully, the application templates provided in Expression Blend and Visual Studio make this a lot easier because the elements in the templates already conform to this grid.

Clean and Consistent Typography

One of the most important parts of a design that focuses heavily on typography is the consistent use of a set of font faces, weights, and sizes. Because the majority of the design will be type, the information hierarchy will be conveyed mostly by font weight and size. Headers, subheaders, section headers, and body type should all be easily distinguishable from one another through the use of some combination of font weight and size. For example, a header might have a very large font size to set it apart from other text. Subheaders could be in a smaller font size but still large enough to indicate that they are headers for a section of the design. The body type will tend to be of a weight and size that is comfortable to read.

Applying Typography to Running Total

Windows 8 defines what is called a type ramp. The type ramp identifies the font size, weight, and, in some instances, color to be used for all cases in the application. For example, the page header for an application page should use the Segoe UI Light font and a font size of 42pt. A subheader on a page will also use Segoe UI Light, but with a 20pt size instead. All items that are used in UI layout will use the Segoe UI font family. It is the most recognizable font in Windows 8. In Figure 1-5, you'll notice how this font is applied in the Running Total application.

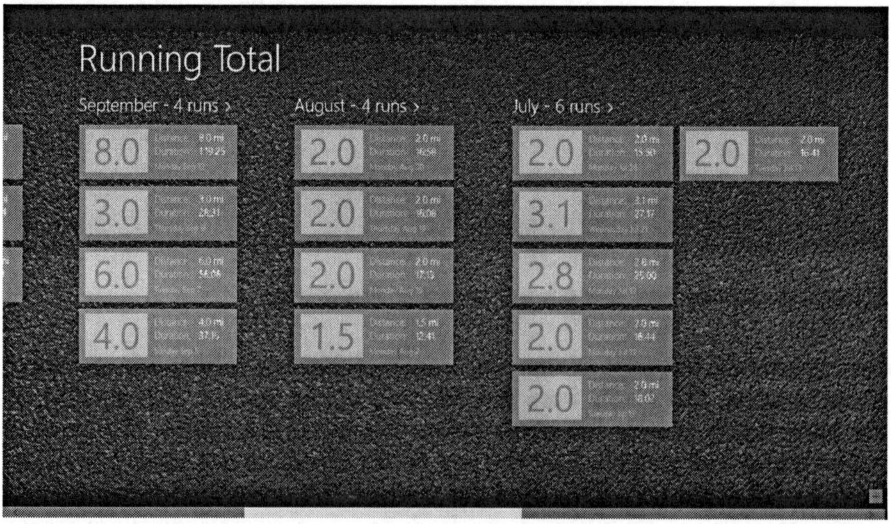

Figure 1-5. Screenshot of Running Total with a selection of font sizes and weights

The most important thing to note is that the variety of font sizes and weights helps the content stand out and reinforces the information hierarchy of the application. Since there is very little chrome in a Windows 8 application, this use of typography becomes really important. Following the font guidelines for Windows Store applications will ensure that your application provides an experience that fits the rest of the operating system. Again, the templates provided by the developer tools make this easier for you. Almost all of the text styles you will ever need in your Windows 8 application are defined for you in the styles provided by the templates. All of the default text that is provided in the templates is already styled using these guidelines.

Clear Iconography

Another feature of the International Typographic Style is the use of clearly understandable iconography. Consider the previously mentioned signage that is used throughout the world. Most people recognize the male and female symbols shown on signs indicating restrooms. They may not be able to read the text that appears alongside the icons, but they will still know which door leading to the restroom that is appropriate to them. The icon clearly depicts this concept. There is a very distinct minimalism applied in the construction of the icons used in this type of signage. The icons in this style tend to use a single color and very simple curves and angles.

Applying Iconography to Running Total

Windows 8 has a much cleaner design style than previous versions of the operating system. Gone are the shadowing and gradient effects on toolbar icons. Windows 8's closest feature to a toolbar is the app bar at the bottom or top of the screen. Following is an example of an app bar from Running Total (see Figure 1-6).

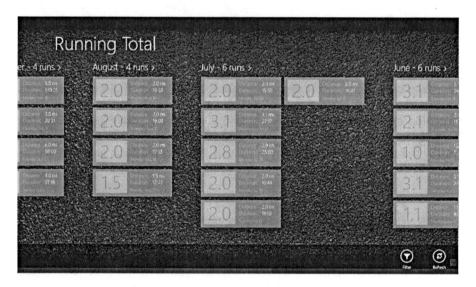

Figure I-6. Running Total's app bar with Filter and Refresh commands

Notice how instead of the traditional icons one might expect in a toolbar, the app bar contains single-color icons housed within a circle. These cleaner icons are intended to convey their behavior without a lot of visual noise. This is very similar to the use of icons on signs such as those I discussed in the previous section. It should immediately be obvious what the icon for the app bar button does. In the case of Running Total, the Filter icon is a clean representation of a funnel. This is a very common icon for filtering. You will need to find or create clean icons such as this for any buttons you need in your app bar. Thankfully, there are numerous icons provided for you in the Segoe UI symbol font that ships with Windows 8. Many common icons can be found in this font, and there are guides for how to use them in app bar buttons. Take advantage of them!

Use of Photographic Imagery

One of the most compelling features of some designs that follow the International Typographic Style is the use of photography. In general, designs in this style favor the use of photography over illustration. This use of photography adds a certain amount of liveliness and personal connection to the design. A poster for a symphony might feature a large violin rendered in detail and accompanied by text that tells the viewer when and where the event is being held. The information is important, but it is the image of the violin that draws attention. It will still be the photograph that elicits the emotional connection to the design, even one that is perfectly laid out and accompanied by beautiful text that is aligned perfectly to a typographic grid. As someone who is designing something, you want to create the same connection to your design.

Applying Photographic Imagery to Running Total

In Windows 8 applications, the use of photographic imagery is encouraged for all applications where it makes sense to use it. Images can be used to great effect as the background for an application page (see Figure 1-7). This type of use can reinforce branding or simply fill up white space in a manner that is meaningful.

Figure 1-7. Running Total's landing screen features vivid photographic imagery

One of the best examples of the use of photographic imagery is the suite of applications that were created by the Bing team and ships with Windows 8. These applications include News and Sports and a few others. The key defining feature of these apps is the large graphic that takes up a good portion of the top-level screen. It is a feature that really draws the user into the application from the very first launch. I wanted to capture that same feeling in the Running Total app, so I brought this feature along. The photograph on the top-level screen of Running Total shows a running shoe on a track. The colors in the shot are amazing, and the theme for the application is captured in the big, bold image. It is not always necessary to use very large photography such as this, but when it makes sense to do so, it can certainly make an impact. Other uses of photography you might consider in your application include photos to represent items in your application (see the News app for great examples of this) or in your app's tile. Whatever you do, you should definitely include photography in your application, if appropriate.

Bold Use of Color

The bold use of color is another strategy employed by the International Typographic Style to attempt to draw attention to the design. Whether used as a background upon which the typography is laid or as the accent color for the text, the goal remains to draw the user in. Though there are many posters in the International Typographic Style that use grayscale, most use very bold colors to make key parts of the design stand out. The creative use of bold colors adds personality to a design.

Using Color in Windows 8

As a platform, Windows 8 encourages the use of bold colors. Simply taking a look at the default tiles that ship with Windows 8 reveals a variety of different colors. It's a good idea to carry this design concept into your app as well. For Running Total, the color scheme is partially derived from the photograph used for the launch screen. The pinks in the graphs in that section of the app are based on the pink hues in the running shoe. It doesn't really matter what color scheme you choose for your app, but be consistent with it. The default templates that are provided by Visual Studio and Expression Blend are very plain, with just black and gray hues. Treat them as a blank canvas that should be painted with the colors you choose for your app. The resulting application will be much more visually appealing.

Cinematography and Motion Design

One final major influence on the Windows 8 design style is cinematography and motion design. The best examples of the combination of these disciplines are the opening sequences of movies. It's somewhat of a lost art, but at one point a lot of movies included an opening sequence as the credits rolled. The sequence was often animated and had a theme consistent with the plot of the movie.

Saul Bass is regarded by many to be the master of this art. He created opening sequences for many Alfred Hitchcock movies, such as *North by Northwest*, *Vertigo*, and *Psycho* in addition to many others. Bass is credited with having created opening sequences for films between 1954 and 1995. The sequences he created reflect the plot through his use of animation and imagery. For example, for the movie *Anatomy of a Murder*, he creatively used cutouts of body parts and animated them around the opening credits. The opening sequence to Hitchcock's *Vertigo* was referred to by Martin Scorsese as "a mini-film within a film." This is a pretty accurate statement when you consider the fact that Bass creatively distilled the entire plot of the film into a two-and-a-half-minute title sequence.

The goal of this type of title sequence was to create an emotional connection with the viewer before the film begins. Saul Bass explained this concept best when he stated:

> *My initial thoughts about what a title can do was to set mood and the prime underlying core of the film's story, to express the story in some metaphorical way. I saw the title as a way of conditioning the audience, so that when the film actually began, viewers would already have an emotional resonance with it.*

Creating this type of "emotional resonance" is something you should aim to do with your design. Creations enlivened with motion and dynamism have a much better chance of establishing personal connections.

Motion Design in Windows 8

Windows 8 provides numerous opportunities to use motion design to capture your user's attention and create an emotional connection to your application. Subtle animations are used throughout the operating system as a way to guide the user's eye and to keep applications lively. The development tools for Windows 8 also include an Animation Library, which you can use in your application to ensure that the animations you add to your application match those used by the system. This means that with a few simple lines of code, your app will provide an animation experience that is consistent with other applications developed by Microsoft and other developers.

The Saul Bass quote about establishing an emotional connection to a movie before it even begins is instructive. You have the opportunity to do that with your application designs and can carry that momentum throughout the experience. It all starts with the initial screen of your app. In a traditional application, you might never think about animating your application's launch; however, a subtle animation on app launch can really catch the user's eye the first time he or she uses your application. Download and take a look at the Cookbook application that is available at the Windows Store. On the first app launch, the app needs to initialize the recipe data. Instead of statically doing this with a progress bar dialog box such as we might have seen on Windows 7, the creators of Cookbook decided to include the animation of a beautiful large picture of some asparagus and then have a progress indicator that animates. When the download is complete, the asparagus dissolves, and the main screen of the app emerges. What could have been a boring launch sequence suddenly becomes an engaging first-launch experience that makes the user want to dive in to the rest of the app to see what it can do.

Another place where animation plays a big role in bringing users to your application is in the Live Tile. Many Live Tiles cycle through information and images. It's a subtle effect, but it is the animation that really draws attention to the tile. Great examples to look at to see this effect in action are the Travel, Finance, Weather, News, and People applications that come with Windows 8. They are constantly updating with information. It keeps the Start screen fresh and dynamic. The more useful information your tile can animate through on a regular basis, the more likely the user is to keep your application pinned in an easily viewable location on their Start screen. I'll go into more detail about Live Tile design in Chapter 6.

Summary

In this chapter, you've taken a tour of some of the inspirations that were fundamental to the creation of the Microsoft Design Style. You have learned about the focus on minimalism that was a characteristic of the Bauhaus movement and saw how it can simplify our applications. You then explored the clean typography and bold use of colors of the International Typographic Style and looked at how that style contributes to the character of Windows 8 apps. Finally, in the discussion of cinematography and motion design, you learned how these concepts can keep your applications feeling alive and dynamic. In Chapter 2, I'll introduce the five principles that guide successful Microsoft Design Style and show you how to employ them in your app design.

Microsoft Design Style Principles

The guiding force behind all successful Windows 8 application designs is what is known collectively as the Microsoft Design Style Principles. These five principles are the foundation on which a successful app should be built. The Microsoft Design Style Principles reinforce the design fundamentals presented in Chapter 1 and introduce some new concepts in addition. While the principles may seem similar to marketing phrases, they are absolutely essential both to understand and incorporate into your app design. The Microsoft Design Style Principles are the following:

1. Show pride in craftsmanship.

2. Be fast and fluid.

3. Be authentically digital.

4. Do more with less.

5. Win as one.

I will introduce each of these principles in order, and as I do, I will also tie the concepts to our ongoing sample Running Total. I hope that applying the principles to our real-world example will help you understand how to apply them in your own work.

PRINCIPLES, NOT MARKETING PHRASES

It bears repeating that the five principles listed above are not marketing speak, even though they may seem to be at first. When I initially heard these principles while attending BUILD 2011 sessions, I thought they sounded like a bunch of buzzwords. After learning their importance, however, it began to make sense to me why they are expressed as they are. The whole purpose of marketing phrases is for them to stick in your mind. If you can attach some meaning to a phrase, and that phrase can stick in your mind, you are much more likely to think about the associations you've attached to the phrases when the time comes to apply them. So, bear with me. I promise to attach some meaning to each of these phrases so that they can stick in your mind for beneficial reasons rather than because they recall cheesy marketing speak.

Show Pride in Craftsmanship

Merriam-Webster defines the word 'craftsman' as "one who creates or performs with skill or dexterity." The word craftsman is often associated with physical trades such as carpentry or jewel crafting. However, you can and should treat software as a craft. Craftsmen begin to practice their trades as apprentices and are forever honing their skills in an effort to become expert at their profession. Craftsmen will practice every day to ensure that they are becoming better at what they do. True craftsmen will understand how far they have come since apprenticeship and will apply the knowledge acquired in the past to future endeavors. Craftsmen will use the right tool for the right job to the best of their abilities, in order to achieve the best possible results. Ultimately, it all comes down to pride. The best definition of 'pride' that I have seen that fits this context is "a feeling or deep pleasure or satisfaction derived from one's own achievements." We must be proud of our work. If you treat your software design work as a craft and truly put your best effort into it, it will be hard not to be proud of the outcome.

For Windows 8 and Microsoft design in general, there are some key concepts that arise from this idea of showing pride in craft. The key concepts I'll focus on are the following:

- Sweat the details.
- Make it safe and reliable.
- Align to the grid.

Sweat the Details

When it comes to software design on a platform with a strong design language, it should come as no surprise that details really matter. Taking a look at the vast landscape of applications available for Windows 7 and earlier versions, one can see what happens when there is not a strong sense of design guidance. Traditionally, Windows has not been a place where users of various applications have been able to have a sense of consistency from one application to the next. Sure, within some application suites, such as Adobe Creative Suite or Microsoft Office, there is some level of consistency. However, comparing even those two suites against each other reveals myriad differences in how to design key user functionality. It's not just functionality, however, that suffers from this lack of consistency: the whole design aesthetic suffers as well. From application to application, there is simply no sense of a common personality on Windows 7 and previous versions of Windows. This isn't really a fault of developers or designers. Users simply weren't provided strong enough guidance for newer applications, and older applications with even older design ideas continue to run alongside them. This all changes with Windows 8 and the Microsoft design language.

It's time to care about the details. And not merely care about them, but truly sweat them. There are very strong design guidelines for Windows 8 applications that have been designed to ensure a higher level of platform consistency from application to application. For example, the page header for each application should have a left margin of 120 pixels and a baseline 100 pixels from the top. When you switch from application to application, you can see that the headers consistently align in this location. If you did not pay attention to even this one detail in the design guidance, your application would stick out like a sore thumb. Users will become accustomed to the consistency in the platform, and if you don't sweat every detail in your application design, you may find your application unappealing. Microsoft has provided you with a very good set of design guidelines for your applications to follow, and it is in your best interests to make sure your designs adhere to them.

Sweat the Details in Running Total

Taking a look at the Running Total application, one can quickly get the feeling that the designers spent a lot of time on the details. Many of the colors chosen for the design come directly from the large image that takes up a big portion of the initial screen. The running theme of the application has been reinforced not only by this image but also in the background of the pages (see Figure 2-1). Great care has been taken to ensure that the fonts used in the application are within the set of fonts defined for Windows 8. The designers, both interaction designers and information architects, also thought about what type of data was relevant on each screen and showed only what was most appropriate for each level of the application hierarchy. This type of attention to detail is very important when building Windows 8 applications.

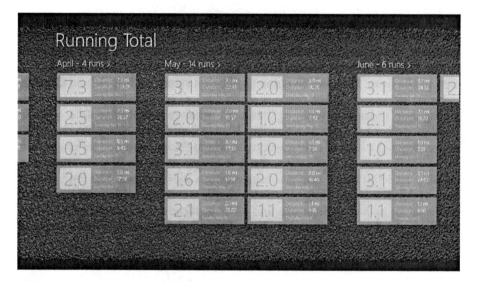

Figure 2-1. Road imagery in background reinforces running concept

Make It Safe and Reliable

As I mentioned in the previous section, applications have had very inconsistent user interfaces in previous versions of Windows. For instance, one area of applications that has a wide amount of variance in previous versions of Windows is the concept of Settings. I say 'concept' because even the word used to describe this in applications may vary between Settings, Options, Configuration, and so forth. Where is this functionality found in your favorite applications? Is it under the Tools menu? Maybe it's under the Edit menu, or the File menu? What happens when you click on it? Maybe it pops up as a modal dialog box. Or, it might change the whole screen to show the options or settings. The point is it's inconsistent. Users do not know with certainty where to go to configure things from one application to the next. Users can be much better served, and Windows 8 provides the necessary tools.

The Windows 8 design guidelines call out locations where, for example, Search, Settings, and application commands should go. I will discuss these in detail in Chapter 4, but the key point here is that it is very important to make sure you're putting things in the right place. The goal should be consistency with the platform, such that your app does not seem foreign to users. They are going to expect to see Search functionality under the Search charm and Setting under the Settings charm. If you attempt to do things in a different way, you risk confusing your users. Confused users are not likely to continue to use your app, and they probably won't recommend it to their friends either. It is a blessing that Microsoft has provided such strong platform guidance. Take advantage of it, and make sure your application fits the platform.

Making Running Total Safe and Reliable

In terms of making your applications safe and reliable, it comes down mostly to putting common functionality in the right places in the app. For instance, it is possible to search the runs that are saved by Running Total. Rather than implement a custom search box within the main user interface screen of Running Total, the app integrates with Windows 8 using the Search contract. Users of Windows 8 will quickly learn that Search functionality on Windows 8, both at the system and application levels, is performed through the Search charm on the right-hand side of the screen (shown in Figure 2-2). As a designer, you only need to figure out how to display the results that are returned by the application. You do not need to design custom search dialogs, because Windows 8 handles that in a consistent pane invoked through the Search charm. Since users of your application will have learned the Search charm through their use of Windows 8, they will already know how to search your application. As an added benefit, any time a user searches from anywhere else in Windows 8, your application will show up in the list of apps that can be searched, because you have implemented the Search contract.

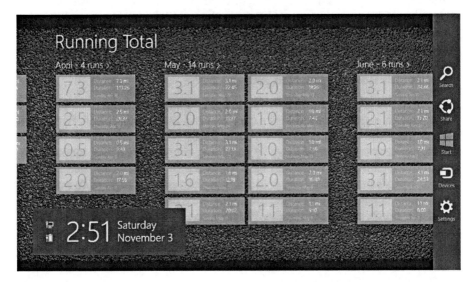

Figure 2-2. Charm bar

Another common user task that Running Total places in a consistent location is Settings. As I mentioned in the previous section, Settings functionality has often been placed in very inconsistent locations from application to application. In Windows 8, Settings can be accessed in all applications by tapping the Settings charm. When tapped, a pane will animate from the right-hand side of the screen (referred to as a "Settings flyout") with a list of Settings categories for the app. Tapping one of these categories will show the settings for this category. Navigation within the pane will allow the user to go back to the category list. For Running Total, the settings include account-related information, as well as information about the application.

Having predefined locations to put common functionality allows developers and designers to create experiences that users will have a much easier time learning. Skills learned in one part of the system can be applied to other applications. Users will have a much stronger feeling of confidence as they learn these key concepts.

Align to the Grid

What will require the most sweating of the details in your application is aligning to the Windows 8 design grid. Platform consistency is extremely important, and one of the easiest ways to be inconsistent is not to pay attention to every little detail in the grid guidance. The design guidelines call out very specific locations for the elements of your user interface. I will discuss the major alignment guides in Chapter 4, but the key here is that, at least for now, these should be treated more like rules than guidelines. There will come a time when a designer may creatively break the Windows 8 design grid, and it will amaze and delight. For now, it is much more important for you to strive for consistency between apps, and the easiest way to do that is to stick to the grid that Microsoft has provided you.

Aligning to the grid has some benefits above and beyond platform consistency. Alignment to a grid makes things easier to read and comprehend. For example, compare the newspapers of the early 1900s with those today. In the early 1900s, newspapers were laid out by hand, and there were major inconsistencies in the alignment of the columns. They were very difficult to read because of this. Today's newspapers are created using computerized page layout tools. This results in a much more readable experience because the layout and alignment are much more consistent. Modern tools make this possible. When developing for Windows 8, you have the benefits both of a modern platform and modern tools. The templates that come with Visual Studio make it easy to align to the Windows 8 design grid, because all of the rules are baked into the styles that come with them.

Aligning Running Total to the Grid

The Windows 8 typographic grid defines a common structure that is easy to spot as you switch from app to app. The easiest places to see this grid in action are the application title and the content region (the main area of the screen). I have annotated the application title and content region in Running Total in Figure 2-3.

Figure 2-3. Margins indicating title and content regions

The application title is located 120 pixels from the left edge of the screen with a baseline of 100 pixels down from the top edge of the screen. The top of the content region is 140 pixels below the top of the screen. If you switch between various applications, you will see that all apps (that follow the design guidelines!) conform to these basic rules. If your application title deviated even a few pixels from these rules, it would be immediately apparent. Following the typographic grid will allow you to create an easy-to-understand information hierarchy. Therefore, aligning to the grid not only makes your application consistent with the rest of the system but also makes it much easier to use!

Be Fast and Fluid

If you heard any of the Microsoft Design Style Principles before, it was very likely this one. In fact, "be fast and fluid" was repeated so frequently during BUILD 2011 that there are drinking games related to it. That being said, there is a reason the phrase was stated so many times at that event. "Fast" refers to responding quickly to user interaction. "Fluid" refers to the way in which the application responds and displays information to the user. Being fast and fluid is a core part of the Windows 8 personality. Interactions are responded to immediately, and the application flows from one screen to the next with animations that visually tie one portion of the experience to the next. The most important components of being fast and fluid on Windows 8 follow:

- Design for touch.
- Delight with motion.
- Be responsive and ready.

Design for Touch

I will discuss the details of designing for touch in Chapter 5, but for now it is important to understand why this concept is so essential to Windows 8 application design. Windows 8 applications are designed to be touch first. This means that you have to take comfort and ergonomics into consideration when designing your applications. Since it would be very easy on a tablet to make a lot of assumptions regarding what is ergonomically feasible in a user interface, Microsoft took the time and effort necessary to research this subject. The metrics such as those shown in Figure 2-4 are the result of extensive usability testing and exercises.

Figure 2-4. Application with thumb area overlay

The preceding image shows the areas on screen that users were able to reach with their thumb while holding a widescreen tablet in landscape orientation. The center section of each thumb region is the area the average person can reach with minimal stretching. The outer two bands are areas that are reachable, although with increasing difficulty, in order to hit targets within them. It is important to position content within these regions to achieve maximum ergonomics and comfort.

It is very important not to segregate touch interaction from mouse interaction. You should not design your application such that if it detects a mouse and keyboard, it provides a different way to interact. If the application is properly designed for touch, the mouse interactions for the application will come automatically. There is no difference between a tap of a finger and the click of a mouse other than the extra precision that the mouse pointer affords the user. The event provided to the application is the same, and the behavior for the interaction should be the same. The good news for you as a designer is that you can focus solely on the touch interaction, knowing that you get the mouse interaction as a result.

Designing Running Total for Touch

When thinking about designing for touch in Running Total, there were a lot of things to consider. Because the application is very data intense, it was ensured that data could be presented in such a way so as to be easily manipulated and explored using touch. This starts at the first screen, where a simple pinch gesture activates semantic zoom. Instantly, you are taken from a screen that includes a lot of data pieces (the individual runs) to a screen that aggregates the data into months. The size of each of the interactive elements in the interface provides more than enough space for a finger to tap it. Touch feedback is provided immediately using either highlighting or tilting of the tapped element. When viewing the individual run details screen (see Figure 2-5), the map and chart that display for the run are able to be manipulated using touch as well. Users can zoom and pan the map using touch. They can also touch to view tooltip information for the chart. All of these interactions are also possible using the mouse, without any custom handling specific to mouse and keyboard. The end result of all of this design work is an application that feels equally capable of performing its intended tasks either through touch or mouse interaction.

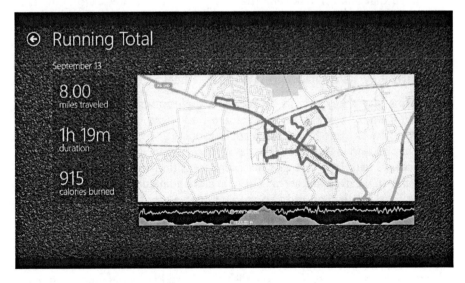

Figure 2-5. Run details screen—map and chart are touch enabled

Delight with Motion

As mentioned in Chapter 1, motion design plays a fundamental role in designing applications for Windows 8. Animations can bring your application to life and add a little bit of flair and make it appear very thoughtfully put together. Animations can help your application tell a story as users accomplish their tasks. Even the most mundane tasks can be brightened up by adding a bit of subtle animation. Potentially even more important is that consistent animations help establish the platform uniformity that is so vital on Windows 8.

Every animation you add to your application should serve a distinct purpose. The goal is not to add animation just for the sake of being fancy but, rather, to help communicate information or activity within the application. That being said, almost every element in your application will animate at some point, simply owing to platform conventions. There are defined entrance and exit transitions for various scenarios, so it is very likely that at the very least every element in the interface will animate into and out of view. If you need to add animations to your application in addition to these, make sure to follow the design guidelines for animation.

The good news regarding animation in Windows 8 is that Microsoft has provided a lot of pre-built animations to help you design applications that fit in with the rest of the system. These animations are scenario-based. What this means is if you need an animation for repositioning an item, there is an animation in the library for this scenario. Other scenarios include showing and hiding panels, transitioning between pages, fading items in and out, and many others. Most of the animations in the Animation Library have configurable options, so that you can fine-tune them to your specific needs. Using the animations from this library will help you provide animations that fit in with the Windows 8 platform.

Delighting with Motion in Running Total

Animations play a key role in Windows 8 applications. They are so important that many of the key animations are built right into the controls that are used to build most Windows 8 applications. For example, when you create an application using the Grid Application template, you will automatically receive a user interface that performs transition animations as you move around the application hierarchy. These are the animations you will see when Running Total is launched and also as you tap on a month or an individual run. Sometimes, you will want to add animations for elements in your interface that were not added by the template. In the case of Running Total, I wanted to provide a custom loading animation after the large image at the beginning of the first page loaded. This was to ensure that there was not an abrupt and jarring loading sequence. To accomplish this, I used a fade-in animation from

the Animation Library. The fade-in animation runs when the image has completely loaded. In XAML, this can be accomplished by defining a storyboard
and including the appropriate theme animation inside of it, for example:

```
<Storyboard x:Name="FadeInStoryboard">
    <FadeInThemeAnimation Storyboard.TargetName="elementToFade"/>
</Storyboard>
```

In WinJS, you can call code like this from your JavaScript as follows: `WinJS.UI.Animation.fadeIn(elementToFade).done(/* perform next actions here */).`

In both XAML and HTML applications, there is a variety of animations that are
available within the Animation Library. All of the animations are preconfigured
with default values that match their usage in Windows 8. If needed, you can
customize parameters such as duration to meet the needs of your application.
The Animation Library is a great place to go for most of the animations you
will need in your application. It is possible to define your own custom animations, but you should check first to see if an appropriate animation is available
in the Animation Library.

Be Responsive and Ready

It has always been important for applications to be responsive to user input.
Users don't like to wait for confirmation that their actions are being processed. This is even more important when working with touch, because the
experience is much more intimate. Users are interacting directly with the
content in the application, and because there is no mouse cursor, one can't
just show them an hourglass (as if that were ever really all that acceptable in
the first place!). Also, given the goal of having a fast and fluid experience, it is
very important for the application always to be ready to accept user input and
always ready to provide immediate feedback.

The most important aspect of being responsive is providing appropriate feedback for user interaction. When a user taps or clicks on an element in the
user interface, it is essential to provide immediate feedback and to begin processing the action. The goal should be for users to be confident that they
have hit the correct target and the application is taking action on that request.
If the result of the interaction is a long process, provide progress feedback
using either the ProgressBar or ProgressRing controls. The application should
never appear to be delayed or blocked by a background process. Users should
always feel that they are in control and have the assurance that their input will
be processed by the application. Ensuring that your application is responsive
and ready is one of the most important aspects of building a fast and fluid
user interface.

Making Running Total Responsive and Ready

Being responsive and ready begins the moment the application launches. Because Running Total relies on data from the Internet, and there could potentially be a lot of data that will need to be loaded, it is important not to immediately load the interface. The reason for this is that the user interface will be bound to the data that is loaded into the application. If you immediately show the interface, this data will not be loaded, and the interface will appear blank and suddenly data will begin appearing. Instead, you can extend the splash screen temporarily and provide a progress indicator, such as, in this case, a progress ring, while the data is fetched. Once the data is loaded, the application transitions to the main screen. At no time are users left in a state where the interface is not ready for their interaction at launch.

After the application is loaded, the mission of being responsive and ready continues with the elements of the interface that accept user interaction. In Running Total, the best examples of this are the individual run tiles on the main hub screen. When one of these tiles is tapped, there is immediate feedback on the tile. If it is tapped directly in the center, it shrinks uniformly, as if being pressed directly inward. If it is pressed on the left or right side of the tile, it will appear to tilt in the direction it is tapped. This effect is the same as the tile interaction on the Windows 8 Start screen. The main goal is to provide instant feedback that the user has interacted with the correct element and that the application has recognized the user's intent correctly. Users will never be left in a situation where they touch an element on the screen and it doesn't respond to them.

Be Authentically Digital

This principle helps to guide the creation of applications that are modern and to shun much of the traditional look and behavior of classic desktop and mobile applications. You live in a digital world, and your applications should represent that. The key elements of "be authentically digital" are as follows:

- Avoid skeuomorphism.
- Use beautiful typography and bold colors.
- Be cloud connected.

Avoid Skeuomorphism

There are platforms for mobile computing that do a very good job of representing digital things in a way that makes them look like objects in the real world. For example, when displaying a collection of e-books, those platforms may choose to show book covers resting on highly detailed wood-grain shelves. There is a term for this: skeuomorphism. Though there isn't necessarily anything wrong with skeuomorphism, it is not an approach that embraces the digital medium as a new canvas. The Microsoft Design Style Principles favor a much more direct digital representation of objects.

Whether or not one agrees with the premise "skeuomorphism is bad," the Windows 8 platform takes a stance on the issue. Instead of trying to make user interfaces mimic the real world, you are invited to let your content shine through the use of beautiful typography and bold colors. This is where knowledge of International Typographic Style comes in handy, because the design style for how to present content in a Windows 8 UI is heavily influenced by that style. Instead of trying to figure out how to represent a real-world metaphor, such as torn paper edges on a calendar (see Figure 2-6), you can spend your time and energy figuring out the best information hierarchy structure for the content in your application. You can focus on making your content clean and readable. In the end, your applications will have a very modern look and feel to them.

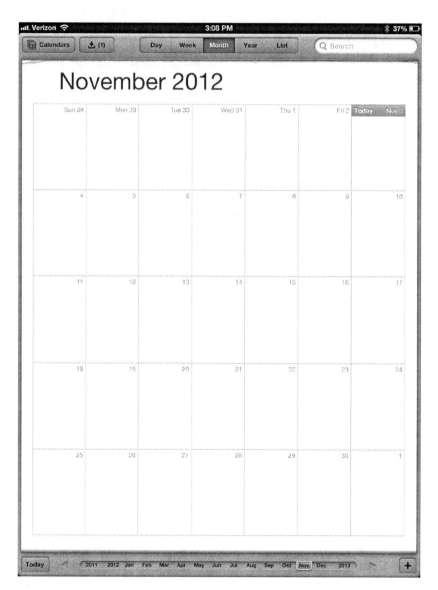

Figure 2-6. iPad calendar is skeuomorphic to the core

Avoiding Skeuomorphism in Running Total

It would be very easy to get carried away with skeuomorphic elements in an application such as Running Total, because there are many physical elements in the subject matter. For example, we could represent the individual runs as running shoes. Put simply, we just avoid that in the application. Note, however, that the background of the pages in the interface has a street texture. This could be considered by some to be skeuomorphic, but I do not consider the use of textures in this manner to be so. This approach is consistent with the use of photography as background imagery in Windows 8 apps.

Use Beautiful Typography and Bold Colors

Instead of focusing on finding cutesy uses of real-world elements, designers of Windows 8 applications are invited to create clean, modern-looking applications. These applications celebrate typography, bold colors, and, often, photography. These concepts should be familiar to you because they are the same concepts informing the International Typographic Style, which was covered in Chapter 1. Where appropriate, applications should favor photography over illustration and focus on clean iconography for buttons in the app bar. The Windows 8 design style guidelines call out a set of font faces (Segoe UI primarily, except in a few cases), font sizes, weights, and colors that should be used in various application scenarios. Using the right font in the right place definitely helps your application fit in with the rest of the apps on the system and also helps establish the information hierarchy within the app. The use of bold colors is highly encouraged in Windows 8 applications. These colors really stand out on the screen and, if used correctly, can really reinforce your app's content and branding. If you don't have a lot of photography in your app, try to find a few colors that work well with your content, and use them consistently throughout the application.

Beautiful Typography and Bold Colors in Running Total

Running Total starts off with a bang, with bold colors and beautiful typography enhancing the large imagery and graphs of the opening screen. One of the colors the app uses prominently (the pink color found in the charts) is derived from the color of the running shoe in the photo. The blue color used in the tiles is a good match for this color and is a blue that has been a staple in this modern style of apps since Windows Phone. It meshes well with the company's branding, so that's why I chose to use it. You should look for ways to tie your color choices to the branding in your applications as well. As for the typography in the application, I have stuck to using Segoe UI fonts in the ranges specified in the design style guidelines. I have annotated some of the font choices in Figure 2-7.

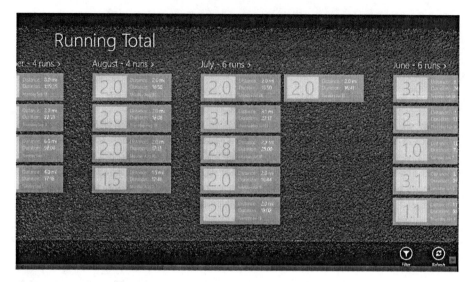

Figure 2-7. Fonts used in Running Total's hub screen

Be Cloud Connected

Another way in which Windows 8 applications are "authentically digital" is their recognition that devices today exist in a digital world. Modern users often have more than one device on which an application can be used. These devices are usually connected to networks and the Internet. Thus, the concept of cloud connectedness can play a big role in application design. Users will expect their data to be available on all of their devices without them having to figure out how to sync it themselves manually. At the very least, account settings for apps should use the roaming settings objects Windows 8 provides developers. When users connect their Microsoft account to their login, these settings will automatically be applied to all of their Windows 8 machines. If you design your application with this in mind, users will not need to enter their credentials on every machine they use your application on. Features like this go a long way toward ease of use and make your application more likely to be recommended to others.

Cloud Connectedness in Running Total

Running Total provides an interesting case study in that the data it renders lives in the cloud. Since that data is already persistent in a known location, you don't need to worry about saving space for the user in that sense. Instead, to embrace the cloud connected aspect of being "authentically digital," Running Total uses Windows 8 roaming settings to put the user's login token for the HealthGraph API in the cloud. This will allow the user to use the application on other machines without needing to authenticate with the service. Running Total also preserves the filter settings the user has set up in the app so that those are available on other machines as well. These two features provide for a user-friendly experience when moving from machine to machine.

Do More with Less

This principle is all about focus. So often in traditional application design, we tend to lose sight of what is important in the application. So much time is spent on making the buttons look right, building navigational chrome, and trying to figure out what commands to add and where to put them. We spend so much time on the things that surround the content that we end up not celebrating the content of the application the way it deserves to be celebrated. I've mentioned the phrase "content before chrome," and this principle is the driving force behind that notion. Doing more with less can be broken down into a few key areas, as follows:

- Be great at something.
- Put content before chrome.
- Inspire confidence.

Be Great at Something

Your application should be great at helping your users accomplish something specific. That seems like a very obvious point, but it is alarming how often applications are allowed to drift from being great at one thing in order to let them be mediocre at a lot of things instead. In Chapter 3, I'll discuss some tactics to help achieve making something great a concrete and attainable goal, but for now, it is important to understand why that goal is important in the first place.

When an application isn't focused on accomplishing a very specific task or addressing a very specific need, it is very easy to begin to add additional features to it. Pretty soon, a button for all sorts of related but arguably unnecessary tasks is included. Lost in the shuffle of adding all these extraneous features is a clear focus on what the user needs to accomplish in the first place. On the whole, the application will suffer as a result of this lack of focus. Not only is there the possibility that the user will become lost in a sea of extra buttons, but the developer will have spent time implementing all of those extra features instead of concentrating on the core tasks. Picking one thing to be good at shouldn't be a limiting force but, rather, a focusing force. It is what will allow your application to stand out in a crowd.

Being great at something means that the "something" in your application will be well defined. Because it will be well defined, it should make your job as a designer a lot easier. You can focus on the best way to represent the content that is involved in accomplishing the task. You can spend your time thinking about the best way for the user to interact with this core task rather than spending time trying to figure out what button to hide all the extra features behind. Those extra features simply won't exist.

Being Great in Running Total

Running Total is great at letting users review their running progress, based on runs they've saved to the HealthGraph system using RunKeeper (or other apps that use the HealthGraph API). It provides the user with aggregate totals at the year and month levels, as well as individual run details. All of the features and information provided to users relate to this goal of providing them with the best experience possible in reviewing their running history. What the app doesn't try to do is allow users to add new runs to the database. It also doesn't allow users to watch a run being performed live (something the HealthGraph API does support). It reports calories burned over time and for individual runs, but it doesn't attempt to be a calorie tracker. All of these features would make for great compliments, but they detract from the focus of the application. It would be much better to try to find some integration points with other apps on the system than to focus on these features for Running Total. Try to keep your apps focused on their mission, so they can be truly great at it.

Put Content Before Chrome

Content before chrome is probably the most recognizable mantra of the Windows 8 design style. One of the most noticeable things about the main screen of applications running on Windows 8 is an almost complete lack of buttons, tabs, and toolbars you've grown accustomed to seeing in your computer applications. Most of the screen real estate of a Windows 8 application is dedicated to the content of the application. Compare the user interface of traditional Outlook on the top in Figure 2-8 to the user interface of the Mail application that is included in Windows 8.

Figure 2-8. Outlook vs. Windows 8 Mail

There is a lot of functionality in the Ribbon and other areas surrounding the actual e-mail content in Outlook. However, a lot of that functionality goes unused on a day-to-day basis. It would be even less likely to be used in a mobile context on a tablet. The important part of the mail application is the e-mail itself, and so much of the screen real estate in Outlook is spent on things other than that mail content. Contrast that with the Mail application for Windows 8. The majority of the space in the Windows 8 application is taken up by the mail message the user is reading. All of the extra features that are truly necessary are either in the app bar or in the Settings charm. This allows users to focus on the primary task of reading and responding to their e-mail. You should note that "content before chrome" becomes easier if your application follows the "be great at something" model.

If the majority of the application is taken up by the content, where will all the other functionality go? How will you structure the application navigation scheme without tabs and trees? As I will discuss in greater detail in Chapter 3, there are new paradigms for how to structure your application in Windows 8. Commands that the user will need to access in order to work with the content of the application will go in the app bar at the top or bottom of the application. Search functionality will go in the Search charm. Settings functionality will be placed within the constructs of the Settings charm. All features related to sharing information from your application will use the Share charm. Removing all of these buttons from the always onscreen portion of your user interface gives you more room to dedicate to the real star of the application, the content.

Content Before Chrome in Running Total

Running Total takes content before chrome very seriously. Looking around the application, you won't find a single traditional button, tab, menu, or tree control anywhere on the main screen of the application. Information hierarchy is navigated through semantic zoom and group headers. Individual runs are accessed through tiles that display content directly on them. Searching, sharing, and modifying settings are integrated into their respective charms in the Charms bar. Commands that need to be performed, such as changing filters, can be accessed in the app bar (see Figure 2-9). With these pieces of functionality not on the screen at all times, Running Total is able to dedicate the entire screen to making the run results really stand out. The app is able to show bigger charts, bigger maps, and more data overall without the additional chrome in the way. The result is actually less cluttered, while providing more information, as shown in Figure 2-10.

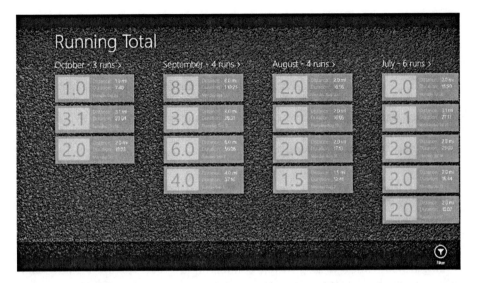

Figure 2-9. App bar

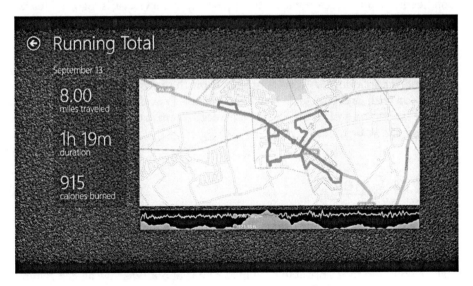

Figure 2-10. Run Details screen uses the full screen to show content

Inspire Confidence

A confident user is a happy user. We've all had that moment when we are using an application and we get totally lost on how to perform a certain task. It is not a very good feeling, and if it happens enough in a given application, it might be time to replace that application with something else. Thankfully, on

Windows 8 there is a well-defined place to put most functionality, and guidelines for everything else. If you've decided what you want your application to be great at, and you've put all of the commands and charm-related functionality in the places they belong, your users will be confident using your app. It is harder for a user to make mistakes when the platform has taught him or her what to expect. If we all play by the same rules when designing our applications, our users will be more confident than ever when using Windows 8. They'll be more likely to try out new applications without worrying that they won't know how to use them.

Inspiring Confidence in Running Total

As mentioned in the "Content Before Chrome in Running Total" section, the app follows the guidelines in determining where to put common functionality, such as Search. In addition to this, Running Total uses Windows 8's built-in Web Authentication Broker when connecting the user to the HealthGraph API. The Web Authentication Broker is a mechanism available to you that allows for the provision of credentials in a safe manner. Any time an application needs to authenticate with a third-party web service, it is a good idea to use this control. This is done to provide the user with the same experience they would have when adding Twitter or Facebook support to the People application on Windows 8. A user that has performed this task in the past will be familiar with what Running Total is attempting to do. This gives a user much more confidence. A confident user is much more likely to explore your application than one who feels timid and unsure. Providing a consistent experience that fits the rest of the Windows 8 ecosystem is the best way to inspire confidence in your users.

Win as One

For the most part, the principles discussed thus far have addressed providing a good experience for your users. The "win as one" principle is mostly about what the platform provides to you if you play along. The concepts in this principle are about making your job designing the interface easier and potentially making your app more profitable. Win as one is about what we all can gain by following the Microsoft Design Style Principles. The key concepts of win as one are the following:

- Fit into the UI model.
- Work together to complete scenarios.
- Use the tools and templates effectively.

Fit into the UI Model

If you have been following the discussion of the previous four principles, you may have noticed a common theme. Woven throughout the other principles has been the ideal of platform consistency. Windows 8 has a very strong UI model with well-defined locations for the most common user tasks. As I have mentioned, there are benefits to making sure your application fits into this UI model. Perhaps the biggest benefit is that new users of your application will already be familiar with how to use it. For example, they'll already know how to search your application's contents, because it will follow the same way they search the system and other developers' applications. Not very many platforms enforce or encourage this level of consistency in the UI model. You can only gain this benefit if you make sure your application fits into the Windows 8 UI model. You already understand the importance of this from the other principles, but I hope you're now beginning to see how beneficial it can be as well. I'll have a lot more to say about how to best fit into the UI model in Chapter 4.

Work Together to Complete Scenarios

If you've ever designed or developed an application that worked with external services in order to share information, you know just how complex this can be. A lot of time and effort might need to be spent figuring out how to work with the SDK or the API for the external service. This is time that is much better spent working on the core functionality of your application. It gets even worse when the external service updates its SDK or API, which will necessitate your having to modify your application for the integration to continue working. Windows 8 provides developers with a much easier path for implementing these scenarios.

Windows 8 provides mechanisms called contracts that allow applications to declare certain capabilities that will be fulfilled by the system. There are contracts for a variety of uses, including Search, Share, and Settings, in addition to many others. The most relevant contract to the win as one principle is the Share contract.

The Share contract allows an application to expose data within its app that can be shared using another app. The Share contract allows an application to declare itself to be either a source for sharing information, a target for sharing information, or both a source and a target. A Share Source application declares a certain type of data as being available to be shared with other apps. For example, a recipe application might declare that it is able to share recipes that conform to a certain schema. A Share Target application declares that it is able to share items of certain types. For example, a recipe might declare that it is able to share URLs or recipes. A Share Source application that shares recipes doesn't need to know anything about the other apps on the system that are capable of sharing recipes. All the Source app needs to do is share those recipes through the Share contract. Compatible Share targets on the user's system will be presented to them when they tap the Share charm with a recipe selected in the Source app. From this point, Windows 8 will pass the data to the target. The target does not need to know anything about the source application. This mechanism eliminates the need to integrate directly with Twitter, Facebook, or whatever social network of the future. As long a developer chooses to share data through the Share contract, it will be able to work with any application on the system capable of sharing that data. This is great for users and great for developers.

Working Together in Running Total

At one of the Windows 8 developer events I attended, there was a session devoted to Contracts in Windows 8. The person conducting the session said something that stuck with me. He said: "Not all apps make sense as a Share Target, but most apps make sense as a Share Source." What he meant was that most applications have some sort of data that can be shared with the outside world. Running Total is not the type of application that will receive data from other applications and share it somehow (that's a Share Target), but it does host a lot of data that its users might want to share with other people. For this reason, Running Total implements the Share Source contract for individual runs. The data that is shared to the other applications that implement Share Target is the URL to the individual run. URLs are a very common type of data shared on Windows 8, and this provides the greatest potential for users to have an application that is capable of sharing their running data on their system. Any app that is a Share Target capable of receiving a URL will be able to share the data that Running Total provides as a Share Source.

Use the Tools and Templates Effectively

Microsoft has provided a great set of tools for building Windows Store applications in XAML and HTML. Visual Studio 2012 is a fantastic code editor, and the design surface for designing XAML user interfaces in Visual Studio has been updated to use the Blend designer. Blend has also been updated for XAML and is brand new for HTML5 as a very sophisticated HTML/CSS editor. These tools provide mechanisms to preview your application in various device sizes and application themes. Use the tools to make sure your application looks right on a variety of form factors, even if you don't have those form factors for physical testing.

Both Visual Studio and Blend ship with a set of application and page templates for Windows 8 apps. You should explore the files that are included in the Grid and Split Application templates to see how an application can be structured on the platform. The default styles that are included with these templates come preconfigured with the correct margins and pixel alignments for conforming to the Windows 8 typographic grid. When you are first starting out with Windows 8 application development (and, honestly, even after you've been doing it for a while), you should use the templates as a starting point. The templates will get you started with the proper alignment of elements and also provide you with the navigation scheme needed to go from page to page. Customize the application and page templates to make them your own, but do yourself a favor and make sure to start from the templates.

Tools and Templates Used to Build Running Total

Running Total was built using the Grid Application template. This is a great example of how you can customize the base template so that it doesn't look much like the original. The benefits you gain from this are the resources that are provided for you in the original template. In terms of tooling, both Visual Studio 2012 and Blend were used, as each tool has its own strengths and weaknesses. Visual Studio is great for code editing, and Blend is a fantastic tool for getting your user interface laid out correctly, both in XAML and HTML. Pick a template that's appropriate for your application and use the right tools for the job, and you'll be off to a great start.

Summary

In this chapter, I introduced the five principles of Microsoft Design Style. These principles are central to successful Windows 8 application design. Since it is important to see how these concepts are applied to real-world applications, I also showed how they are applied in the Running Total reference application. In the next chapter, I will explain some design strategies that will help guide your application design.

Design Strategies for Windows 8

Designing applications for any platform requires proper planning and strategies. Windows 8 is no exception. In fact, given the increased importance of focused application design, I would argue that it is even more important for Windows 8 app design than before. In this chapter, I will outline some key planning techniques and strategies that will enable you to design an application that meets the needs of your users, no matter what type of application you are building. I'll begin with some strategic planning tips that will help you design a very focused app. I'll then move on to some techniques that will help define the user interface of your application. These include not only the static look of the application but also the animations and user interactions. Most of these techniques will revolve around low-fidelity prototyping, but I will also discuss tools that are available for creating high-fidelity mock-ups after preliminaries have been established. The specific strategies I'll be discussing are

- Defining the app's mission through a "best at" statement
- Brainstorming and refining application scenarios
- Choosing a navigation and content strategy
- Prototyping

The "Best At" Statement

Every application begins with an idea. The idea could be to help users solve a problem or just waste time in an entertaining way. Regardless of the goal of the application, however, every idea can and should be solidified into what is known as a "best at" statement. The statement is so named because it is phrased as follows: "My application is the best in its category at _____." The "best at" statement should be a single, focused sentence. Given that all applications will slot themselves into a particular category, it is this statement that will help you define how you differentiate your app from others in the category. This is very important to successful Windows 8 app design, as this "best at" statement will guide all of the decisions that are made regarding what scenarios the application will support and what features it will include. For our Running Total application, the "best at" statement might be: "Running Total is the best in its category at helping runners analyze their running data."

There are two qualities that a "best at" statement must have in order to be successful. The statement must be specific, and it needs to be truly differentiated. Since the "best at" statement will be so essential to the success of your application design, let's take a look at each of these two aspects in detail.

Specific "Best At" Statements

When defining our "best at" statement, it is very important to make it as specific as possible. Because we are basically defining the essence of the application, we will want to make sure we are able to distill it to a goal that communicates exactly what the application will be good at. The language that will specify the app's mission must not be vague or too broad. There is a big difference between "My application is the best in its category at allowing users to browse recipes," which is very broad, and "My application is the best in its category at helping users find recipes that meet their dietary needs," which is very specific. You will want to craft a statement that is much closer to the more specific example.

The reason specificity is so important in this statement is that it is the driving force that will focus the scenario list that will be created in the next step of the design process. If the "best at" statement is too broad, we won't be able to eliminate nearly as many scenarios as we would otherwise. This will make a lot more sense after I have defined the scenario brainstorming and refining process, but just keep in mind at this stage that a specific "best at" statement will result in a much more focused application. Having a focused Windows 8 application is a key to your success.

Truly Differentiating Your "Best At" Statement

Crafting a statement using specific language to make sure it is focused is just half of the battle. It is also very important to ensure that your "best at" statement is "truly differentiated." What this means is that your statement should clearly indicate what makes your application stand out in its category. Here, you are trying to define what makes your application unique. This is what will make users want to download the application and keep using it. There will be a lot of applications in the Windows Store. Depending on what your application does, there may be similar applications competing for your potential users. Your "best at" statement should convey what your app brings to the table that other, similar applications may not. In the case of Running Total, there will probably be other applications in the Store that deal with running data; however, the goal of Running Total is not only to provide access to running but also to help users visualize and make sense of the data. In the preceding recipe example, it wasn't sufficient merely to provide a mechanism to browse recipes. There are probably countless applications that bring this feature set to the table. What sets the app in that example apart is its focus on finding specific recipes that will meet users' dietary needs.

Your first attempt at the "best at" statement might not be differentiated enough. In fact, thinking further about it, you might determine that the preceding recipe example is not sufficiently differentiated for this category. Many applications could provide a feature set that would help users find recipes that fulfill their dietary restrictions. So, one way to refine this would be to identify a specific dietary restriction and focus the app around it. For example, perhaps instead of a generic dietary restriction recipe finder, you could focus your application on gluten-free diets. The "best at" statement might be something such as the following: "My application is the best in its category at helping users maintain a gluten-free diet." Note that some aspects in the scope of the statement may broaden as you hone others. In this case, the scope has shifted from "finding recipes" to "maintaining a diet." This is okay, however, because the other aspect of the statement has narrowed from accommodating all types of diets to focusing strictly on gluten-free diets. Many generic recipe applications will contain gluten-free recipes, but they may not have any tools to help users maintain their diet. Specificity is what will differentiate the application that is built using this "best at" statement. You don't have to worry about adding too many unnecessary features, because in the next stage of design planning, I will only focus on scenarios that fit the "best at" statement.

Real-World "Best At" Example

In one training session where the "best at" scenario was discussed, the presenter offered a real-world example that really stuck with me. I think it is very helpful to look at things outside of the application design context from time to time in order to help clarify any confusion that might arise from focusing too much on concepts as they apply to software design. Many of these concepts can be applied in the real world as well. "Best at" statements have applicability outside of software, because the goal is simply to help determine the focus of whatever it is applied to.

The presenter's example explained the difference in the elements that make up the "best at" statements for a few different types of places where one might go with friends to drink beer. His favorite location for this activity was a pub. A pub is a location where one can go with friends to drink beer that provides an environment conducive to conversation. The lighting is not too dark or too bright. If there is music, it is more of a background element and not so loud as to inhibit conversation. Contrast this with a nightclub. This is another type of place one can go with friends to drink beer. However, the environment in a nightclub is completely different from that at a pub. It might be impossible to conduct much of a conversation in this environment. The focus of a nightclub is much more on music and dancing than on conversation. One last example the presenter offered of a place where one can go with friends to have a beer is Oktoberfest in Munich. The experience there is also completely different from that at a pub. A pub will usually have seating available, but if you want a seat at Oktoberfest, you must show up very early in the morning. In addition, at Oktoberfest, you are not likely to sit around and converse. You are much more likely to stand on your seat, waving a beer stein to the strains of Bavarian music.

The common thread that runs through the three previous examples is going somewhere with friends to drink beer. However, there are many different ways this activity can be approached. The most generic "best at" statement we could make for this, then, is "a venue that is best at providing a place to meet friends for beer." All three of the venues discussed in this section meet those criteria, however, so the statement is not specific enough. Each example requires a more defined "best at" statement to truly capture the goal of the application. A pub would be "best at providing beers in an atmosphere that is good for conversation." A nightclub would be "best at offering drinks as well as dancing." Finally, Oktoberfest would be "best at providing a unique once-a-year opportunity to drink beer while standing and waving a tankard." The "best at" statement you create for your application should distinguish your application from its peers, much in the same way the three preceding venues exemplified are set apart. If you achieve this specificity, it will be really easy for users to understand why your application is best for them.

Running Total's "Best At" Statement

I have mentioned the "best at" statement for Running Total a few times, but I haven't really explained what makes it an effective "best at" statement. The category under which Running Total will be included in the Windows Store will be Health and Fitness. In this category, there are likely to be many other applications that allow users to access their running data. Various applications (such as RunKeeper and Nike+) have established themselves in recent years as great tools for runners to track their runs using their phone's GPS. Most of these applications have rudimentary ways to view the data on the phone itself, and some have fairly decent web sites from which some data analysis can be done. However, most of these services do not have a desktop or tablet-grade application for viewing this data. It is this deficiency that Running Total aims to address. It has access to the user's running data through the HealthGraph API; however, instead of providing only a basic view of this data, Running Total aims to help the user analyze and make sense of it. Pace trends, monthly totals, graphs, and maps all present the data in ways that aid the user in visualizing his or her running data, so that he or she can measure progress over time. As long as the application focuses on these types of scenarios, it will be successful in differentiating itself in its category. That's why Running Total's "best at" statement is "Running Total is the best app in its category at helping runners analyze their running data."

Picking Appropriate Application Scenarios

The next step in designing your application is figuring out the scenarios that the application will support. For the purpose of this activity, we can define a scenario as something the user can accomplish in the application. For example, one scenario for Running Total might be to "view the details of an individual run." As I mentioned in the previous section, we want to make sure that the application scenarios that we support align with the "best at" statement we have defined for the app. Choosing the right scenarios for the application is a three-step process that progressively refines things until we have a list that is completely appropriate for our application. The process basically involves the following steps:

1. Brainstorm all possible scenarios for the app.

2. Remove all scenarios that sound like "features."

3. Remove scenarios that don't align with the "best at" statement.

After completing this process, we will be left with a scenario list that is a perfect fit for our "best at" statement. These scenarios will define the app and will help focus the rest of the application design. This process is as much about figuring out what will not be in the app as deciding what will be in it. When creating an app, we must make sure to focus only on the scenarios that accomplish our specific goal with the app. Feature creep, allowing too many unnecessary features to sneak into the final product, must be avoided, in order to create a useful, unique application. This process is designed to help prevent feature creep.

Brainstorming for Scenarios

Brainstorming is a process that can be very productive, if done well. In scenario brainstorming, the goal is to identify all of the potential things that your application could allow the user to do. At this point, don't worry about whether or not the scenario seems like it might be out of scope. If the scenario includes something that your application could do, write it down. The only "rule" at this stage of brainstorming is that each of these scenarios should describe something a user can do, or *accomplish*, using your application.

Recording every idea that comes into your head in this manner can be very helpful at this early stage. More often than not, this process will result in at least a few scenarios that you might not have considered had you not taken this open-minded approach to gathering them up front. Though the final goal is to have a small and focused list of only a few scenarios, you will want to take this opportunity to make a comprehensive list of many possibilities. Having all the possibilities laid out like this will ensure that the resulting final list will have the best possible scenarios for your application. You should consider engaging in this process with a team. In many cases, you will be working with a team, even if it is made up of only a few people. It's important to involve other people, so that you can get a variety of ideas. Brainstorming works best when more than one person is involved.

Brainstorming Scenarios for Running Total

Let's take the first step in this process and perform it for our reference application, Running Total. Given that the app deals with data related to running, we know that there will be scenarios involving viewing this data at a variety of different granularities. For example, users might want to view their running totals for the current year, month, or week. It might also make sense for users to be able to share the details of a particular run. On the very ambitious end of the spectrum, we might want to allow users to compare a few running events and provide them the opportunity to compare the runs. These would all be valid scenarios in this early brainstorming process. Something else that might be outside of the scope of the application yet still be valid at this stage would be something like allowing the user to view the running data for a run that is actually taking place. Tracking a live run over the Internet is, in fact, something that is supported by HealthGraph (the back end for Running Total). If you think of a scenario that might be possible in your application, it should be noted in this list. Table 3-1 is a potential scenario list for Running Total.

Table 3-1. Initial Brainstorming for Running Total's Scenarios

View all of my runs	Track nutrition data	Track sleep data
Refresh run list	Compare multiple runs	Quickly see totals over time
Track a live run	Share a run	Compare my running stats with a friend's running stats
Find new places to run	Search for runs	Add data for a new run
Visualize running data	Modify account settings	Find nearby races

Removing Scenarios That Sound Like "Features"

The previous step was very open-ended, without many restrictions on what constituted a scenario that applies to the app. The purpose of keeping it so open-ended is that we are going to make a few refinements to the list to focus it on a small set of scenarios that we will base our design on. The first refinement we will make to our scenario list will be to remove any scenarios in the list that sound like "features." What do I mean by this? An example would be something such as "refresh the data." While this is certainly something the user may need to accomplish using your application, it is more of a feature that helps to accomplish a larger scenario. The goal of the entire process here is to end up with a list that defines the unique tasks our application will have to accomplish. "Refresh" and "search" are generic features that most applications will provide, so we don't need to include them in our scenario list.

Removing "Features" from Running Total's Scenarios

Taking a look at the scenario list for Running Total, we can quickly see that there are a lot of features in the list. Table 3-2 is the scenario list with the unnecessary features crossed out. The resulting list is made up of scenarios that could help define the design for our application. Some of these scenarios may not fit our "best at" statement, but we'll address that issue in the next step.

Table 3-2. Scenario List with Features Crossed Off

View all of my runs	Track nutrition data	Track sleep data
~~Refresh run list~~	Compare multiple runs	Quickly see totals over time
Track a live run	~~Share a run~~	Compare my running stats with a friend's running stats
Find new places to run	~~Search for runs~~	Add data for a new run
Visualize running data	~~Modify account settings~~	Find nearby races

Remove Scenarios That Don't Match the "Best At" Statement

We now have a set of scenarios to work with that could all be a part of an application in the appropriate category for our app. However, many of these scenarios are likely to be out of alignment with the "best at" statement we created in the first step in this process. Since we have defined the "best at" statement to be the guiding principle for our application design, it is very important to refine the list to remove any scenarios that don't match up with the statement. If a given scenario in the list doesn't clearly help to accomplish the vision defined in the "best at" statement, then it needs to be removed from the list. The result of this will leave us with a very focused set of scenarios that should serve as a great starting point for our design.

Aligning Running Total's Scenarios with Its "Best At" Statement

When conceiving scenarios for Running Total in the previous phases, I introduced many that are definitely outside the scope of the "best at" statement. This should happen in any successful brainstorming session. If you aren't generating ideas that might push the boundaries of your app scope, then you might miss some great ideas. Those ideas might not find their place in the app you are designing right now, but they might be the starting points for future designs or iterations of the current app. For now, though, these ideas must be removed from the list of scenarios for Running Total. Some examples of features that might fit the category of app we are building but are outside the scope of the "best at" statement include live tracking of runs, tracking nutritional data, and tracking sleep data. The first scenario would be great for an app that is used to track a street team during a marathon, but it doesn't really fit our vision of an individual runner analyzing his or her past running performance. The latter two scenarios would be a better fit for an application that helps runners determine the impact sleep and nutrition has on their running performance. These scenarios are definitely valid for our target category (running/fitness apps), but they aren't a great fit for the "best at" statement.

A few of the items I removed require some further explanation. Ultimately, I wanted to end up with two or three scenarios when finished. Typically, this means the list has been refined sufficiently to assure a focused first version of an app. I removed "Add data for a new run" because all of the run data in the initial concept is being synced from an online resource (runkeeper.com). "Compare multiple runs" is a scenario that could be very valuable for an application of this type. It is the last scenario I removed in order to get down to the three scenarios that best defined the application. It is a scenario I would probably want to add to the application, but I'm not sure it is essential to the application on its initial release. Table 3-3 shows the scenario list after being edited to include only those that align with the "best at" statement.

Table 3-3. Final Scenario List

View all of my runs	~~Track nutrition data~~	~~Track sleep data~~
~~Refresh run list~~	~~Compare multiple runs~~	Quickly see totals over time
~~Track a live run~~	~~Share a run~~	~~Compare my running stats with a friend's running stats~~
~~Find new places to run~~	~~Search for runs~~	~~Add data for a new run~~
Visualize running data	~~Modify account settings~~	~~Find nearby races~~

Now that you've captured the "essence" of the application in this final list, you have a solid guide for what to design through the rest of the process. Keep this list handy and in mind at all times.

Choosing a Navigation and Content Strategy

In the first two chapters of this book, I described the concepts of "do more with less" and "content before chrome." When you successfully apply these ideas to your application, you are left with the task of essentially using every pixel on the screen to present your data. Because many of the traditional application controls, such as menus and search boxes, are no longer on the screen, this presents some interesting new challenges in terms of application structure.

Having this much screen real estate is very liberating, because it makes available for your app's data a lot of the room on screen that would have traditionally been devoted to chrome. However, I can also understand how this additional space may at first seem like a burden. A bit of comfort might result from knowing there will be such things as menus and toolbars occupying the screen. While we're rethinking how to cope with all of this newfound screen space, Windows 8 also invites us to rethink the way we build our information hierarchy. Because we will be moving away from using tabs and trees to present this hierarchy, we will need to provide new ways to navigate through the data in the application. The extra screen real estate also gives us much more room to make the details of our data shine in full-screen glory once the user approaches it. Before we can begin prototyping and mocking up the design for the app, we must consider the navigation strategy. Take a look at the following navigation strategies for Windows 8: the hub and the navigation bar.

Navigation Strategies for Windows 8

One of the most enjoyable aspects of many well-designed Windows 8 apps is how easy and inviting it is just to browse them and interact with their content. Without the burden of tabs, menus, and trees, the content of the app seems much more accessible and easier to explore. Much of this results from the navigation strategies that have been developed for Windows 8 with this browsability in mind. Concepts such as the hub, navigation bar, and semantic zoom allow users to get through the content in an app in a very fluid and discoverable way. For your users to get this experience from your application, you'll need to think about how the content in your application is structured and provide the proper navigation for this structure. Windows 8 apps that span more than a single page tend to use one or both of two main strategies: the hub and the navigation bar.

The Hub

The hub is possibly the most recognizable design strategy in all of Windows 8. This is due in large part to the fact that the Start screen is essentially a hub for your app tiles. The hub is the best tool you have available to you to make your content browsable and discoverable for your users. When utilized correctly, the hub offers a visually enticing and fully engaging content presentation style that truly invites your users to explore your app's content. It's important to understand what makes the hub work before it is possible to take full advantage of what it has to offer. To that end, let's take a look at how an application that uses a hub is structured. Refer to Figure 3-1 as I go through the details of how the hub navigation pattern is structured.

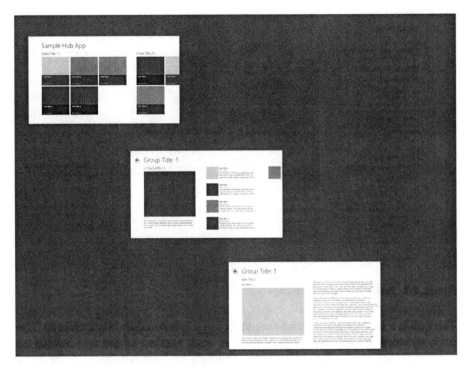

Figure 3-1. Hub application as implemented by the Grid Application template

An application that uses hub navigation has three components: the hub page, the section (or group) details page, and the item details page. The hub is the launching point for the app. An application that uses a hub is broken up into sections, and each of these sections is represented on the hub. For example, in the News application, the groups are the different categories of news that are available to the reader (see Figure 3-2).

BING DAILY

U.S. ›

Scandal widens; US general's emails 'flirtatious'

AP ASSOCIATED PRESS
42 MINS AGO

The sex scandal that led to CIA Director David Petraeus' downfall widened Tuesday with word the top U.S. commander in Afghanistan is under investigation.

Clinton says his foundation to tackle health gaps

REUTERS
3 HOURS AGO

The new Clinton Health Matters Initiative will try to close the gaps in health based on income, race and education, and also take aim at preventable disease.

Soda wars: Cities seek restrictions, taxes to curb obesity

ATLANTA JOURNAL-CONSTITUTION
7 HOURS AGO

Long Islanders fume over utility's storm response

AP ASSOCIATED PRESS
8 HOURS AGO

While most utilities have restored electricity to nearly all their customers, LIPA still has tens of thousands of customers in the dark.

Pockets of Misery Persist after Hurricane

THE NEW YORK TIMES
15 HOURS AGO

POLITICS ›

Post offers hint of GO path

WSJ THE WALL STREET JOURNAL
4 HOURS AGO

As Republicans grapple with how to adjust their party's long-term strateg choice over a House leadership post could provide an early signal on whic way it is headed.

Congress begins session with budget catastrophe looming

AP ASSOCIATED PRESS
27 MINS AGO

Secret of the Obama Victory? Rerun Watchers, for One

THE NEW YORK TIMES
17 HOURS AGO

Last Updated 3:12 PM

Figure 3-2. News application hub page

The hub is a navigation scheme that structures information hierarchically. The basic strategy for the hub page is to have each section of the app bubble up some content to the hub. You want the hub to have a subset of the total content of the app that allows the user to explore the entire app before tapping on anything. The navigation from the hub takes one of two paths. The user can tap on one of the section headers, which will navigate to the section details page. He or she can also tap on an individual item, which will jump them directly to the details for that particular item.

The section details page presents all of the items for a given section or group in the application. Because the goal of the hub is to allow for exploration and entice the user into exploring the application in greater depth, it can only show five to ten items for each section. The section details page, on the other hand, is the place to show all of the items for a given section. For example, the News application shown in Figure 3-2 typically shows a maximum of six items for a news category. However, tapping on "U.S." navigates the user to the U.S. news section, revealing all of the news articles about the United States (see Figure 3-3).

Figure 3-3. News application "U.S." section details

At this level, the application can either lay out the individual items similar to the way the hub did, or it can do something creative with the section content (more on this in "Running Total's Hub"). As in the case of the hub, tapping on an individual item initiates navigation to the item details page, which shows more content about that particular item. The section details page also has a back button that can be used to navigate the hierarchy back up to the hub page.

After tapping or clicking on an individual item from either the hub page or the section details page, the user will be taken to a page offering additional details for the item. This page is ultimately what represents the data in your application; it's the reason the user is using your app in the first place. In the News application example, this would be the page on which the user reads a specific article (see Figure 3-4).

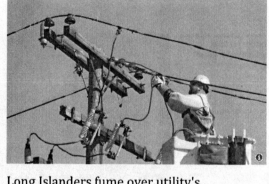

Long Islanders fume over utility's
storm response

AP ASSOCIATED PRESS

Figure 3-4. A specific article in the News application

The only navigational chrome that is present on the item details page is the back button, which will take the user either to the section or the hub, depending on how he or she navigates to the details page. It's important to take advantage of the lack of chrome and use the full screen to present the content on this screen. Notice how the article in Figure 3-4 uses imagery and text to fill the screen with the contents of the article. If the purpose of the hub and section pages is to allow the user to explore what the app has to offer, the item details page is where you deliver on the promise of the "best at" statement.

Structuring the information hierarchy to fit into the hub navigation scheme requires some careful planning. Many traditional applications have complex navigation schemes that may include a complex hierarchy with multiple levels of nesting. The information is often hidden under tabs or navigational trees. Users are typically presented with only one type or category of information at a time. This limits the amount of exploration a user can undertake. Contrast this with the hub, at which all of the sections of the app are viewable for perusal. The hub scheme requires a flattening of the hierarchy in the application, so that a glimpse of all of the sections of content is visible at the top-level hub. This flattening of the hierarchy is what allows for easy exploration of your app. What may not be apparent from the screenshots is that the hub is a long, horizontally scrolling screen, intended for users to explore in order to find content. A few representative items from each section can be shown on the hub, to encourage further exploration into that section.

If you choose to use a hub in your application, you will need to analyze your content to determine which sections are necessary to include. After determining which sections to include, you should prioritize them by placing the sections you feel the user will use most often closer to the beginning of the hub. Since you can use semantic zoom to allow users to jump anywhere in a long hub, they will still have easy access to the less relevant items. (See Figure 3-5 for a look at how the News application uses semantic zoom to enable quick jumping across the hub.)

Figure 3-5. Semantic zoom in the News application

The final question you will have to resolve is how to represent your items in each level of the hub navigation scheme. As you move through the hierarchy, you will have increasing amounts of space to devote to details concerning the items, and the only restriction to how you present the data at each level is your own creativity. Running Total puts a unique spin on some of these concepts, so let's take a look at how Running Total uses the hub.

Running Total's Hub

The content of the Running Total application lends itself perfectly to using a hub. The data in the hub that will be presented to the user will be related to the running activities he or she has logged in the current calendar year. A feature could be added to the application to allow the user to view another year's runs, but this didn't make it into the initial version. At a high level, it makes sense to break down the year into months. So, the months become the sections. The hierarchy for Running Total will then be the hub (year), section (month), and individual run detail (day). For the hub level, the app shows a maximum of ten runs per month, which can each be tapped on individually to view the run details. This allows the users to get a glimpse of their running activity over time, without too many details. The left-most section of the hub also has an overview dashboard, which gives some quick summary totals. Panning to the right, the user will be able to browse through all of the months in the current year. See Figure 3-6 for a look at the top-level hub of Running Total.

Figure 3-6. Running Total's top-level hub

One of the more unique design decisions made for Running Total is evident in the section details screen. Rather than present the month view in the same way as the hub, it was decided to stay true to the "best at" statement and bring some data visualization to this view. Any successful section details screen should allow access to all items within the section. It's okay, however, to get creative with how to represent this. For Running Total, the decision was made to represent the days of the month as items in a column chart, where the height of the bar represents the number of miles run on that day. Tapping on a column in the chart will initiate navigation to that run's details. It's a potentially unexpected twist on the typical section view that really adds personality to the Running Total design. In addition, some month totals were added to the top of this section to mimic the yearly totals from the hub. See Figure 3-7 for an illustration of the section details screen of Running Total.

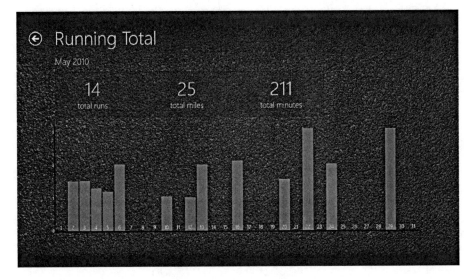

Figure 3-7. Running Total's monthly view page

For the individual run details page, we really wanted to deliver on the promise of the "best at" statement. That meant that we needed to provide good data visualization for the running activity being viewed. The map at the top of the screen shows the route that was taken on the run. The chart at the bottom corresponds to the elevation and average pace over the course of the run. To tie the two together, touch and mouse gestures on the chart are used. Moving the mouse or panning over the chart with a finger will control a circular marker along the path of the run. This marker is synchronized with the position of the cursor on the chart. This provides a visually engaging and fun way to interact with this representation of an individual run. See Figure 3-8 for a look at Running Total's individual run details view.

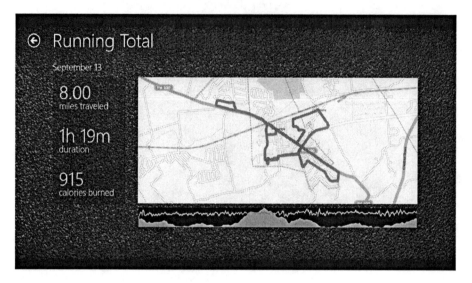

Figure 3-8. Running Total's individual run details view

The Navigation Bar

The navigation bar is the second major navigation technique that can be used in Windows 8 applications. Similar to the app bar, the navigation bar lives just off the top edge of the screen and is made visible using the same edge gesture as the app bar. Unlike the hub, which is used for hierarchical navigation, the navigation bar is used primarily for flat navigation structures. This means that when selecting one option from the navigation bar, there is not typically a back button to return users to where they previously were in the flat navigation structure. You can treat this flat hierarchy usage of the navigation bar almost as "modes" of the application.

A prominent example of the use of the navigation bar can be found in the Windows Store version of Internet Explorer. Internet Explorer uses the navigation bar to display the browser tabs that would traditionally occupy space on the browser at all times (see Figure 3-9).

Figure 3-9. Internet Explorer uses a navigation bar for browser tabs

This is in line with the concepts we discussed in the previous chapter related to allowing the full extent of the screen to celebrate the content that the user is most immediately interested in. By moving all of the typical browser chrome off-screen, the Windows Store version of Internet Explorer has the distinction of being the first browser to default to a full-screen view of web pages instead of to a confined window. To create a new tab in Internet Explorer, the user simply invokes the navigation bar, by swiping from the top or bottom edge, and then taps the "+" button. All of the tabs opened are represented in the navigation bar in a visual fashion and can be tapped to access. Note that when a tab is tapped, the back button will navigate within that tab, not back to the previous tab, just as with a normal browser. This is a flat hierarchical use of the navigation bar, where each tab is a distinct section of the app.

More Advanced Uses of the Navigation Bar

In its simplest incarnation, the navigation bar is used as a mechanism to navigate between sections of a flat hierarchy. If you read the design documentation provided by Microsoft, this is the extent to which the company describes how a navigation bar can, and, perhaps, should, be used. For example, in the original versions of the Bing News application, the navigation bar had very simple entries for "Bing Daily," "Sources," "My News," etc. It was a very flat list that was intended to switch between different viewing modes of the application. These modes were only accessible from the navigation bar, so it was a concept that was very easy to understand. The latest versions of Bing News and Bing Sports offer a much more feature-rich navigation bar that breaks the norm. Because the Bing apps were commissioned to be examples of what best-of-breed applications could look like for different categories of applications, what has been done with the navigation bar concept bears mentioning.

Instead of a flat set of "modes" to put the application in, the navigation bar in the new versions of the Bing applications combines the previous concepts of modes with an expanded role for the main section of the app. For example, in the main portion of the Bing Sports application's navigation bar, there is a set of buttons that corresponds to each sport that is available in the application. Each of these buttons contains a drop-down arrow that, when tapped, reveals the sections contained within that sport. With this design, it is possible to jump straight to the NFL players portion of the app right from the navigation bar (see Figure 3-10).

Figure 3-10. Bing Sports application's navigation bar allows for easy content switching

This type of functionality allows the user to jump across the application very efficiently. I might want to check scores from this weekend's football games and then jump to the most recent hockey news. Using the improved navigation bar design, I am one swipe and two taps away from these very disparate concepts. Other areas of the app can be navigated in the traditional flat mode of operation, but it seems that the main-intended-use case of the navigation bar for these apps is this quick jumping across the traditional hierarchical structure of the app. Even the back button operates as one would expect, as long as the navigation bar is used to navigate within the main "Sports" section of the app.

This new use of the navigation bar is something I haven't been able to find documented anywhere. To me it feels a bit like taking the classic navigation one might find on a web site and making it presentable in a touch-friendly way. To that end, I think this usage of the navigation bar is good for applications with lots of content. It simplifies the navigation stack by allowing users to jump between pieces of content they are interested in without having to navigate through the complete application hierarchy.

Use the Navigation Bar as Needed

To this point, every time I have introduced a concept, I have shown how it was implemented in Running Total. However, Running Total does not use a navigation bar. The navigation bar is great for switching modes (or other similar navigational concepts), and in the first version of Running Total, it really only has one mode. Since there is no navigation bar to show in the application, I thought it might be instructive to determine when it might be appropriate to add a navigation bar to Running Total. One thing that we could add to the application to help runners stay on track might be some tips based on data we have collected from the HealthGraph API. Information such as current body weight, sleep totals, and caloric intake are all available from the HealthGraph API if the user has decided to track these. For users who are tracking these data points, we could choose to provide some analysis for them. Maybe their pace and total distance are better when they've gotten a lot of sleep and eaten a certain amount of carbs. With the right data presentation, this could make a runner more successful once he or she understood it.

However, this type of data is very different from what we have been providing so far in the application. The main portion of our app is dedicated to showing yearly, monthly, and individual run data. To introduce this new functionality, it would probably be most appropriate to make it a separate section of the app that can be accessed through a navigation bar. Because the app is not very deep, we would be using the navigation bar as a mechanism to navigate a flat hierarchy with two options: Activities and Analysis. We could create an icon to represent each of these options and then add them to a navigation bar. For your application, you'll want to determine whether a navigation bar makes sense and add it only if truly necessary.

Prototyping Your Design

At this point, we have gone through the key concepts regarding application structure, so you probably are beginning to get an idea of what your application might look like. Now is a great time to start prototyping your design to make sure you capture and explore these ideas fully before you begin to implement them in your app. Doing this up front can save you a lot of time and effort if you happen to catch some design flaws or new ideas now instead of later. The cost of finding flaws increases the further along in the process you are. Prototyping may even lead you to discover that your application needs to go in an entirely different direction.

THE IMPORTANCE OF PROTOTYPING

If you are a developer, it is very important to resist the urge at this point to just start coding. There is a tendency to want to just jump in and get things working, with the thought of coming back to the design later. It is essential to ignore this tendency. Your implementation work will be much more useful to the app as a whole if the design of the application has been fully ironed out before you begin coding. Features such as data representation, content structure, and navigation flow can change dramatically in the prototyping stage, and these demand different needs from the application code. So, take the time now to get things figured out before you write any code. You will thank yourself later.

There are numerous strategies for prototyping and mocking that can be employed for designing Windows 8 applications, and I'll cover a few in this section. Each prototyping strategy has strengths and weaknesses, so you will want to consider using multiple tactics. The prototyping tactics I will cover are

- Sketching
- Paper prototyping
- Digital prototyping
- Visual design mock-ups

Sketching

Sketching is often what first comes to mind when we think of prototyping applications. There is an inherent simplicity in using paper and pencil to capture ideas. Because the main goal of sketching with respect to prototyping is to capture ideas, it does not matter whether you are an "artist" or not. Anyone can create basic sketches. It is actually important to not focus on making the sketches too detailed. The simpler the sketch that explains the concept, the better. The benefit of this to a person who is not fantastic at drawing is that, usually, not much more than simple shapes, boxes, and lines are required. Thankfully, most people are capable of drawing these.

Strengths of Sketching in the Prototyping Process

One of the greatest strengths of sketching is the minimal amount of tools required to start the process. Although there are special notebooks, stencils, and paper templates that can be employed in the sketching process, all you really need to get started is a blank sheet of paper and a pencil with a good eraser.

Possibly the strongest benefit of sketching is the lack of emphasis on details. Details often get in the way of the thought process. We concentrate too much on making things look right and lose track of whether or not our idea is good. Sketching allows us to focus on quickly capturing the ideas to be evaluated. Set the details aside for the time being and return to them later in the prototyping process. Also, because you aren't focusing on getting every single detail correct, sketching is incredibly fast and efficient. It is a good place to start, because you can whip up a bunch of sketches in no time, compared to trying to make a Photoshop mock-up.

Sketching is also very easy to undertake as a collaborative process. Whether sitting around a shared sheet of paper or working on a whiteboard, sketching facilitates discussion, as people can take turns commenting on or adding to existing sketches. Often, this collaboration can be the difference between a successful and a less-than-successful app design.

Another benefit to making sketches is their portability. If I want to share my sketches with colleagues, I can take them to their desks or scan them and circulate them via e-mail. I don't have to worry about file formats or technology stacks. Paper is the ultimate cross-platform tool. It is also easy to dispose of and makes it easier to get a fresh start. Don't like the current idea? Just throw it away! (In the recycling bin, please.)

Weaknesses of Sketching in the Prototyping Process

Although sketching is a great starting point for prototyping, it does have some weaknesses. The biggest drawback of sketching is that, by itself, it is a very static representation of a set of concepts. Although we can arrange sketches in such a way as to show application flow and structure (more on that in the "Paper Prototyping" section), it is very difficult to convey these concepts with sketches. Sketching does not convey animation, because it is just a static drawing. Because the main focus of sketching is to temporarily set aside the notion of caring about the details, it's worth noting that this is also a weakness of sketching that will have to be compensated for by using other techniques. Almost none of the visual design will be decided through sketching. All of these shortcomings are overcome by the use of other pieces of the prototyping process, so sketching should still be the first step in the process.

TOOLS FOR SKETCHING WINDOWS 8 APPS

While sketching can be performed with a simple blank sheet of paper and a basic pencil, there are some tools that may help you in sketching your Windows 8 ideas. Here are some of the products that have been created to help with this process:

- Windows 8 Sketch Pad (`http://www.uistencils.com/products/windows-8-sketch-pad`)

- Windows 8 Stencil Kit (`http://www.uistencils.com/products/windows-8-stencil-kit`)

Paper Prototyping

Paper prototyping is an evolution of the sketching process we discussed in the previous section. Due to the prolific use of basic rectangles in Windows 8 applications, it is actually a very strong candidate for paper prototyping with some very simple tools. All you will need to add to your arsenal from the previous section are some stacks of colored sticky notes. I was first introduced to this concept by Sara Summers, a User Experience Evangelist from Microsoft, who is intimately familiar with the Windows 8 design process. Sara's techniques for Windows 8 paper prototyping use sticky notes as building blocks for the sections on the screen. For example, a basic tile in a Grid Application could be represented by a single sticky note. Cut a sticky note in half, and you have a canvas properly sized for a toast notification. Combine multiple sticky notes to create content sections that are larger than a single tile. Because sticky notes are easy to place and remove from pages, you can "animate" them from one page to the next very easily.

Strengths of Paper Prototyping

Paper prototyping adds some interesting scenarios to the prototyping process. One of the benefits of paper prototyping is reusability. When sketching, if you want to reuse a portion of your sketch in another screen, you will have to redraw that section on the new screen. For example, if you have a toast notification that can appear on different screens, and you want to show what it would look like in context, you will have to draw it on each screen while sketching. With paper prototyping, you have only to draw the notification on a sticky note, and then you can overlay it on any screen on which you want to view it in context.

Sticky notes have the benefit of being very easy to move around. This opens up a lot of possibilities in the design process. When you sketch something but don't quite have the layout or structure right, you often have to create a whole new sketch to capture the idea correctly. For example, if you were designing an application that had three sections, and you drew them in the "wrong" order for good design, you would probably have to sketch that screen again. With paper prototyping, you could capture the sections on sticky notes and try different ordering simply by rearranging the sticky notes until you achieved the order that felt right.

Paper prototyping shares the potential collaborative nature of sketching. In this regard, it feels more interactive, however. If one person on the team wants to try a different layout for a particular tile, she can just draw it on a sticky note and overlay it on top of the existing one. The two can be compared in context by simply placing and removing the options onto the prototype. Whenever consensus has been reached on which should be used, the other can either be thrown away or filed for future reference.

Sketching is unable to convey animations and transitions in a suitable manner. While paper prototyping is still a somewhat static representation of the app design, there are some techniques that will at least allow for some transitional exploration. For example, if you create a cutout that represents a Windows 8 tablet that allows paper to slide through it, you can create a prototype that contains transitions from one "screen" to the next or "animate" individual elements by sliding them around the paper. While completely manual, this process will at least allow you to explore how users move from screen to screen or how objects animate within the application.

Weaknesses of Paper Prototyping

While paper prototyping is a very strong tool for the Windows 8 design process, it is not without a few weaknesses. Paper prototyping does require a slightly larger investment than sketching. You will need to purchase sticky notes and, probably, some folders to contain them in. Transition simulation will also require the creation of a cutout. While more interaction scenarios can be tested this way than in sketching, there are still aspects of the design that can't be tested using paper prototyping. The main elements that are difficult to design for using paper prototyping are animation timing and UI interaction. These are shortcomings that can be overcome with digital prototyping, which is discussed in the next section.

Digital Prototyping

Digital prototyping is the first prototyping technique that requires the use of computer software. The reason digital prototyping and visual design mockups (covered in the next section) should be avoided until later stages of the design is to limit the amount of precision details you are tempted to worry about. Once you start using digital tools, there is a constant temptation to get design features to look just right, down to the pixel. While this is possible in the digital prototyping process, you will still want to avoid getting too picky about the details, such as color choices and sizing. These can be tweaked later, either in the prototyping tool itself or in a mockup created in a graphics editor.

What Is Digital Prototyping?

Before getting into how to choose a prototyping tool, it is important to understand what digital prototyping offers. Digital prototyping allows you to overcome a lot of the shortcomings you faced when using sketching and paper prototyping. For example, most digital prototyping tools contain a set of objects that you can use to easily create the elements for your screen, such as buttons, labels, etc. This saves some time and removes some of the anxiety for those who are less adept at drawing. Many digital prototyping tools also provide ways to transition between the screens in the prototype. This will allow you to finally test those animation timings and transition sequences, to get a feel for how the app will flow from one screen to the next. Using a sophisticated prototyping tool will also allow you to test the interaction design of your app, such as what happens when a user taps a particular element on screen. With the right tool, all of this can be done without writing a single line of code and with sufficient ease of use by designers and developers alike.

Choosing a Prototyping Tool

As I mentioned in the previous section, there is a variety of digital prototyping tools on the market today. You will have to consider the feature sets of the various products as well as determine if they fit your work-flow style and preferred platform. Many of these tools offer free demos, so you'll want to explore them until you find the right one for you.

Some tools are best suited to static mockups that don't contain animations or sophisticated transitions. These tools are basically a digital evolution of the sketching and paper prototyping process. They add the benefit of easy reuse and reorganization, but they still lack the interaction design and animation components that are missing from sketching and paper prototyping.

One tool that addresses these shortcomings is Indigo Studio, from Infragistics. It is my tool of choice when working on digital prototypes, and not just because I work for Infragistics. Indigo Studio was designed to enable easy interaction design and animation. For example, say I want to add a button to my screen (see Figure 3-11). When this button is clicked, I want a label that says "Hello World" to appear. This is as simple as dragging a button onto the screen, then clicking the button and indicating that I want to edit the click interaction.

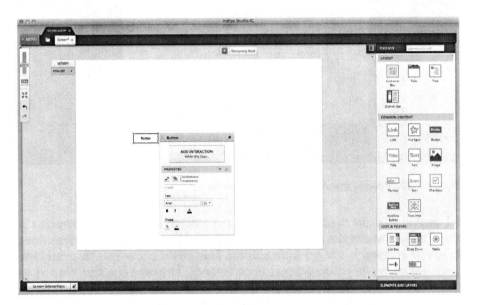

Figure 3-11. Editing a button's click interaction in Indigo Studio

I can then add the label and set its text to "Hello World." If I run the prototype at this point and click the button, the label will appear (shown in Figure 3-12)! Simple, quick, and zero lines of code.

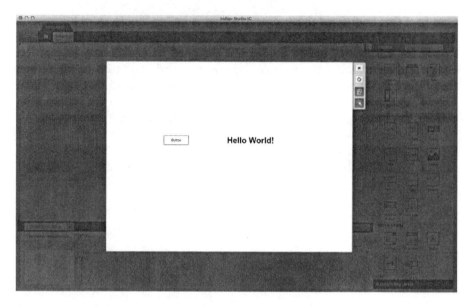

Figure 3-12. Running the prototype in Indigo Studio

If I wanted to make the label fade in, it is as simple as increasing the duration in the time line where the label is added. Indigo Studio also allows for transitions between screens based on interactions. This could allow you to prototype your hierarchy navigation or app bar commands. The time line also allows you to prototype the subtle animations that make for a wonderful Windows 8 app experience. I have designed a few Windows 8 prototypes (see Figure 3-13 for an example) in Indigo Studio, and I hope you'll give the tool a try.

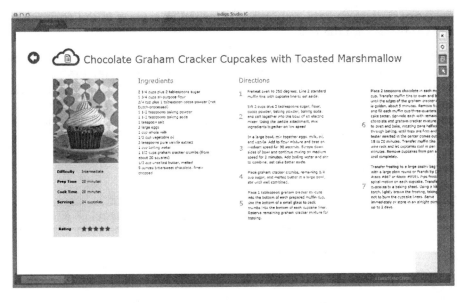

Figure 3-13. RecipeLater prototype

Strengths of Digital Prototyping

Digital prototyping is a very good next step, after you have solidified your ideas using sketching or paper prototyping. It will allow you to bring those ideas to life, using interaction design prototypes. This will allow you to test your design with potential users without writing a single line of code. You can make your prototype look as plain or as detailed as required (within the limits of the prototyping tool), and if the tool allows for it, you can test animations and transitions as well. Most digital prototyping tools also allow for easy sharing in a variety of formats. The greatest strength of digital prototyping is that it produces the closest thing to an actual app you can get without actually building the application. This means you can test all aspects of the design.

Weaknesses of Digital Prototyping

There are some weaknesses with digital prototyping that you have to bear in mind. First and foremost, the level of detail you can achieve creating with a good prototyping tool can be a distraction. In my personal experience, there were a few times during the digital prototyping stage of an app that I spent way too much time getting the colors and alignment just right. While this is important at some point during the design process, letting it happen too soon can get in the way of designing the core features of the app. You should postpone perfection until you have prototyped all aspects of the application and are happy with the results.

Digital prototyping tools, even the most intuitive ones, involve a bit of a learning curve. You will have to learn what types of things the tool can import, what the easiest way to draw certain types of elements is, how to animate things, etc. It can be a lot to learn, and this takes away from the time you have to design and build your application. I would recommend taking the time to learn one or more of these tools, however. It will be a slow process at first, but over time, you will become comfortable with the tool, and your productivity will increase.

TOOLS FOR DIGITAL PROTOTYPING

- Balsamiq (`http://balsamiq.com`)

- Axure (`http://axure.com`)

- Indigo Studio (`http://www.infragistics.com/community/blogs/ambrose_little/archive/2012/08/22/sneak-peek-indigo-studio-by-infragistics.aspx`)

- SketchFlow (`http://www.microsoft.com/expression/products/SketchFlow_Overview.aspx`)

Visual Design Mock-ups

Once you have gone through the prototyping process using the various techniques described in the previous three sections, you will have a pretty solid idea of the information architecture and app flow. You may have even begun to capture some of the visual design concepts, if you utilized digital prototyping tools. At this point, you can finally transition into thinking about the nitty-gritty details of the visual design. These are the details such as color choices, imagery, and alignment that might have gotten in the way of your design thinking earlier in the process. Now that you are comfortable with the design, you can safely begin to work on these aspects. If you are a developer, and graphics tools such as Photoshop aren't your thing, now is the time to consider whether or not you might want to hire a visual designer. Some apps will require only a few color choices here and there and some images. Other apps will require a designer to work his magic to provide a branded experience. Whatever the case may be, the visual design mock-up process will allow the final visual character of the app to be determined. It may be possible to do this within the confines of a digital prototyping tool, if you used one.

Some sophisticated (although often avoided in Windows 8) styling, such as drop shadows or gradients, may not be possible in those tools, however. In such cases, you'll need to use a graphics editor to get the look just right. Taking the time to do a visual design mock-up such as the one we executed for Running Total (see Figure 3-14) will provide a great visual reference as you begin the development of your app. Throughout its development process, you can gauge the quality of your app against this reference point.

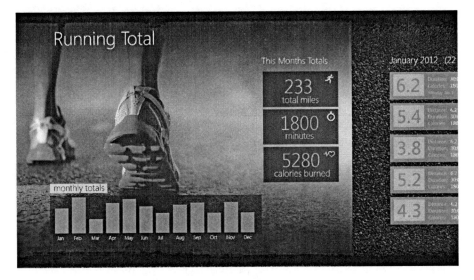

Figure 3-14. Running Total's visual design mock-up

Summary

In this chapter, I introduced some key design strategies for Windows 8. I defined the "best at" statement and explained how a good "best at" statement helps determine what features to include in an app. I walked through the process of brainstorming scenarios for your app and how to refine them based on the "best at" statement. I discussed the two primary navigation methods for Windows 8 apps, the hub and the navigation bar. Finally, I provided an overview of the different types of prototyping techniques and how to use them in your design process. In the next chapter, I will go into detail about how to make sure your app fits into the Windows 8 ecosystem.

CHAPTER 4

Basic Building Blocks of Windows 8 Design

In the first three chapters of this book, you were introduced to the fundamentals of the Microsoft design language and explored some design strategies to help guide your design process. At this point, we're ready to get down to some nuts and bolts of Windows 8 application design. The various controls available in WinRT provide the building blocks we will use to create our applications. Understanding the types of controls that should be used in specific situations and the process involved in designing them are essential to good application design. As discussed in the "show pride in craftsmanship" principle (see Chapter 2), choosing the right tool for the right job is a major key to success.

The interface components that we will use to build our apps can be broken down into categories in a variety of ways. The categories I will choose are based on their location on screen. In this chapter, I will introduce the following major concepts:

- Main content area: the GridView (ListView in WinJS)
- The bottom edge: App bar
- The right edge: Charms bar
- Semantic zoom

Main Content Area: The GridView (ListView in WinJS)

One of the most recognizable controls in the Windows 8 toolkit is the GridView in XAML or the ListView in WinJS when used in its horizontal grid format. I will refer to these controls collectively as "GridView" from here. Because, by its nature, the GridView presents a set of content as a bunch of cells (or "tiles"), this type of layout is sometimes disparaged as giving Windows 8 a very boxy appearance, with all apps looking the same. I think this impression results from too many applications following the base Grid Application template and with only very minor adjustments to the look and feel provided by the template. This is unfortunate, because the GridView can be customized to avoid this monotony. In this section, I'll provide some tips you can follow to ensure that your GridView designs stand out from the crowd and break the basic template mold in ways that add value to your design. Because most apps use a GridView in their main hub, it is important to understand what you can do to use it to your advantage. My suggestions, however, are not mandatory and may not be appropriate for some applications. You should treat them as inspirational starting points for further exploration.

Use Imagery in Your Grid Items

Beginning with the Grid Application template (shown in Figure 4-1) in either Visual Studio or Blend for Visual Studio is one of the best ways to create an application that uses a GridView. However, some design decisions that were made in the creation of this template start developers and designers off in the wrong direction. The most troublesome issue I find with this template is the choice of colors. The black background and various shades of gray coloring the items are uninspiring at best. The intent was to make the template resemble a blank canvas, one that would be augmented with your items, but it doesn't invite developers to create great-looking applications.

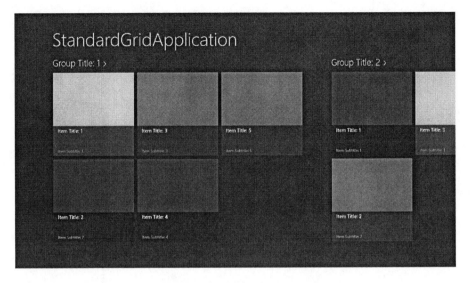

Figure 4-1. Default Grid Application template with gray boxes

Illustrating the impact of imagery in the GridView is the Better Grid Application template shown in Figure 4-2. Here, I wanted to create a template that shows developers what a Grid Application could look like if it made good use of imagery throughout. I started with a light background and used stock images for the placeholders. I think this gives developers a much better first impression of what to create with the Grid Application template. It is also a great illustration of the impact imagery can have in the design of your GridView.

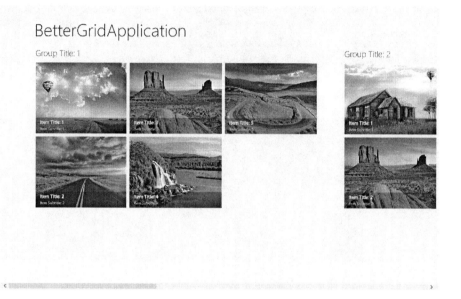

Figure 4-2. Better Grid Application template with colorful imagery

As another example of the effective use of imagery, I prepared an example called TopFlix. TopFlix highlights the most popular movies available on Netflix over the previous year, grouped by genre. The most obvious representation for a movie is the image appearing in its promotions and on its DVD case cover. You can see these represented in Figure 4-3.

Figure 4-3. TopFlix uses DVD case art imagery for its GridView tiles

Images make the content in your application stand out. Users are much more likely to be enticed into exploring your application if they are drawn to its creative use of imagery. Even if the content in your application is very text-heavy, where possible, you should nonetheless explore ways to add a touch of imagery in the GridView to accompany it.

Vary the Size of Your Tiles

This is probably the tip that will have the biggest impact on your GridView design. The best way to break the monotony of an interface with a bunch of tiles that are the same size is not to have all of the tiles be the same size! This strategy works best for applications with hubs having tiles of unequal importance. Many applications use this strategy to create a spotlight, or featured tile, that is very large, alongside other tiles that are smaller in size. One application that uses this to great effect is the Windows Store application shown in Figure 4-4. Notice how the different sized tiles add character to the app.

Figure 4-4. Windows Store uses tiles of multiple sizes

Each item in the GridView can be a variable size that is based on multiples of the base item template. If you take the "Top free" item as the base size, you will find four different item sizes. The width of the "Top free" item is the column width of the GridView, and the height is the row height. We will call the size of the "Top free" item 1x1 (1 row x 1 column). The "NASA Be A Martian," "LivingSocial," and "Office Depot" items are all 1x2. The "Khan Academy" item is 2x2, and the "iCookbook" item is 2x4. All of these items conform to the grid as a multiple of the base-sized element in the grid. The effect of the different sizes helps guide the user to what is important or featured in each section of the application. Get creative, and use this effect to avoid the monotony of the standard grid, where everything is the same size.

Explore More Creative Layouts

There is no requirement that GridView layouts must always use boxy-looking tiles with fairly standard-looking section headers. In fact, I would be willing to bet that a lot of successful applications will not feature this boxy, formulaic look. Instead, many apps will push the boundaries to feature more unique layouts. Take a look at the Tweetro application, for example (shown in Figure 4-5). The content in this application deals with Twitter, so it is very text-based. It would not really make sense for the developers of this application to have followed the traditional tile look and feel of the GridView. Layouts such as Tweetro are possible with the GridView, so keep this in mind as you design your application. You are not restricted to the "squares everywhere" approach to Windows 8 design.

Figure 4-5. Tweetro's layout abandons the boxy tiled look

Another application that abandons the typical look of the GridView is the Bing News application (shown in Figure 4-6) that has been used for many examples throughout this book. Again, the text-based nature of the app lends itself to exploring creative ways to lay out the information. The team that built it also did a great job of integrating images into the layout. The result is very reminiscent of a digital newspaper. Newspapers and magazines can be great inspirations from the print world. Both of these formats are laid out using very strict grids. Even allowing for the limitations of a strict grid, you will find many examples that creatively adhere to this format. Explore these to find some good ideas to use in your application.

Figure 4-6. Bing News lays out its content in a format similar to a newspaper

The Bottom Edge: App Bar

The app bar is essentially a toolbar of buttons that is located just below the bottom edge of the screen. It is where you will place the commands in your application that are not related to Search, Share, or Settings. (Those will go in the Charms bar as we will see later.) The user can invoke the app bar on a tablet by swiping up from the bottom edge or down from the top edge of the screen. On a mouse-and-keyboard setup, the user can right-click anywhere on the screen to bring up the app bar. This is similar to the way users invoke context menus in traditional Windows applications, and the similarity is intentional. There is also a keyboard combination that will show the app bar: Windows+Z. Commands in the app bar can either be global (e.g., "Refresh") or contextual, based on a selected item in the application (e.g., "Delete").

Determining Which Buttons to Include

The app bar works best when it is not crowded with too many buttons. There is a decreasing level of ergonomic comfort the farther a button is from the left or right edge of the device. This means it is essential that we include only buttons on the app bar when/if we actually need them. Depending on the functionality in the application, we may also want to group some buttons under a single main button on the bar. We can use a refinement strategy similar to that we used for application scenarios to ensure we end up with the minimal set of app bar buttons required for all the functions we need in our app.

Step 1: List All Potential App Bar Functionalities

Similar to the application scenario brainstorming we did in Chapter 3, in this step, we want to list every possible command we think we might need in the app bar. It is okay if we end up not needing some of these, or if some ultimately get combined. The main purpose for now is to make sure we explore all the possible buttons we might want to include. It can help to think of these in terms of functional groupings.

For example, let's create a list of potential app bar buttons for the hub page of a fictional app that allows runners to find racing events in their vicinity. Each event in the app will contain a location, a price, a rating, and the distance that will be run in the event. The app will have the ability to display the races as either a list or as markers on a map. We will concern ourselves only with the hub overview page, but a similar process would have to be performed for the section and details pages as well.

We would need app bar buttons that switch between displaying the races in a list or on a map ("List view" and "Map view"). We also have a button that allows the user to re-search the map after she has manipulated it ("Search map"). For filtering the items, we might offer a variety of options, such as "Filter by location," "Filter by race distance," "Filter by rating," and "Filter by price." We could have similar options for sorting: "Sort distance" "Sort by race distance," "Sort by rating," and "Sort by price." If we are in List view, we might want to have the ability to see where one or more of the races is on the map. We could have a "Show on map" button that would allow for this. We could also allow the user to add a selected item to a "Favorite" list or to pin it to the Start screen ("Pin to Start"). Refer to Figure 4-7 for a full list of the buttons included in this first step of the process.

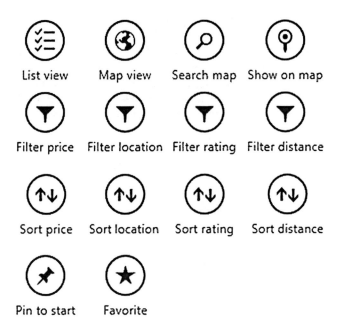

Figure 4-7. Full list of brainstormed app bar buttons

Step 2: Group the Commands into Sets

The next step is to group the app bar commands into functionally related sets. This is so that the app bar will display each set of commands together, separated by a line divider. For our list above, we can group the "List view" and "Map view" buttons together as view commands. We could group all of the filter commands into a set, and the sorting commands into another set. This leaves the "Favorite" and "Pin" buttons, which belong together in a set, because they are related to selection. Figure 4-8 shows the list of buttons grouped into command sets.

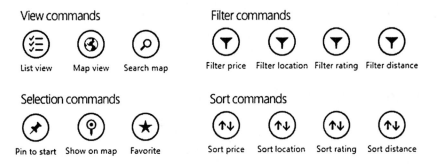

Figure 4-8. App bar buttons grouped into command sets

Step 3: Create Menus Where Appropriate

Sometimes, it is best to combine similar functionality, that is, functions that differ only by one or two parameters, into a menu. For example, we can group our four different kinds of filtering under one button called "Filter." When the user taps on the "Filter" button, he will be presented with a flyout menu that contains the options available for filtering the list of runs (see Figure 4-9).

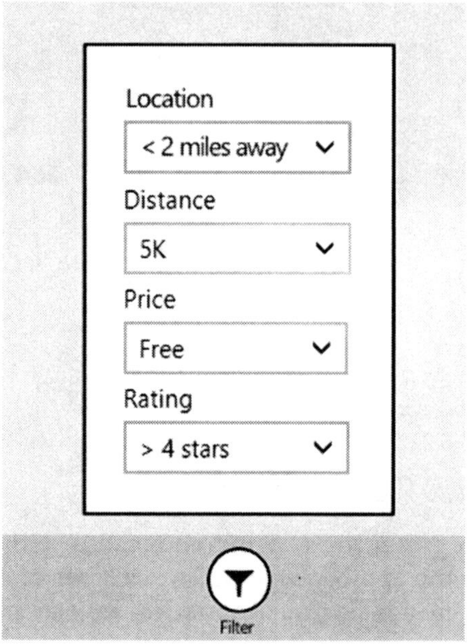

Figure 4-9. Filter options combined into a single app bar button

This provides a few benefits. For one, it reduces the number of buttons we need to display in the app bar. The second benefit is that all of the filtering options can be combined in one place, as opposed to requiring the user to go to four different buttons to filter. We can do something similar with our sorting buttons by combining them under a single button called "Sort." When this button is tapped, a flyout will pop up, containing a list of the sorting options.

Placement of App Bar Buttons

The app bar design favors positioning commands on either the right or left side, close to where the thumbs will be when a device is held in landscape. There are guidelines suggesting the side of the app bar that buttons should be on. We can follow a step-by-step process to make sure we place our command buttons on the correct portion of the app bar.

Step 1: Persistent Commands Go on the Right

The first thing you should consider for each command is whether it is persistent. Persistent commands are always available on a given application screen, regardless of selection or modes on the screen. For our command set, we have three types of commands that are persistent: sorting, filtering, and view-related commands. We will put "Filter" and "Sort" together at the right-most edge of the app bar and then, separated by a divider, "List view" and "Map view" just to their left (see Figure 4-10). You should treat this initial placement on the right side as temporary. For app bars with only a few commands (one to three, as a general rule), you may end up placing persistent buttons only on the right. However, as soon as you have more than three persistent buttons (or more than one command group), things begin to get much harder to reach. At this point you will have to make a shift for ergonomics.

Figure 4-10. Initial placement of the app bar buttons on the right side of the bar

Step 2: Balance the Bar for Ergonomics

If you have more than one command set on the app bar, and they are all placed on one side of the bar, it will be much harder to use them than if you utilized both screen edges. You should attempt to balance the bar, so that you are using the right and left sides of the bar equally. Place the most frequently used commands closest to the edge, so that they are the easiest to reach. For our example, we will move the "List view" and "Map view" button group to the left side of the bar, as shown in Figure 4-11.

Figure 4-11. View commands moved to the left side of the app bar

Step 3: Hide Commands Until Needed

Some commands will only be relevant when the application is in a certain mode. In these cases, we do not want to have these commands taking up space on the bar when they cannot be used. When the application state changes, such that these buttons are now relevant, we will add them to the bar. When adding this type of command button to the bar, we do not want to disrupt the current ordering of the bar. In our example, we have one button that fits this type of scenario: "Search map." This command is only relevant when the "Map view" button is active. When the user is looking at the Map view, we will add the "Search map" button to the right of the view buttons, as shown in Figure 4-12.

Figure 4-12. "Search map" button added when Map view is active

Step 4: Place Selection Commands on the Left Side

Similar to the commands in Step 3, some commands only make sense when items are selected by the user. These commands will always be shown on the left side of the screen. Unlike the commands in Step 3, however, these commands will force any commands that are on the left side to slide over to accommodate them. This makes it easy for the user to see that they have been added to the interface, and they will be consistent with where other apps place selection commands. The commands will be easy to access, because they are close to the edge. Our example has three selection specific commands: "Favorite," "Show on map," and "Pin." When users select a run in the List or Map view, these two commands will slide in from the left, as shown in Figure 4-13. By default, the app bar uses a light dismissal mode. This means that when the user taps on the screen, away from the app bar, the app bar will dismiss. If you need to keep the app bar onscreen, you can set it to be sticky.

Figure 4-13. Contextual commands always appear on the left edge of the bar

Special Command Placement

There are a few commands that always trump the rules above. The most important of these is any command that is used to create or add an item, such as "New" or "Add." This special command should always use the plus symbol and always be at the far right edge of the app bar. Buttons with this functionality are the only commands that may use the plus symbol. If a "Delete" or a "Remove" button is used in tandem with a "Create" or "Add" button, they should always appear directly to the left of their counterparts. One other category of commands that requires special placement is any command that deals with selection, such as "Select all." As with contextual commands that deal with selected items, selection commands should always appear on the left-most side of the app bar.

Icons for App Bar Buttons

Microsoft provides a wide variety of icons that can be used for app bar buttons. These icons are available in the Segoe UI Symbol font in the extended Unicode portions of the font. Thankfully, you do not need to know where in the font to find these symbols, because they have been exposed in a convenient way for both XAML and WinJS applications. In a WinJS application, you can set the "icon" property of an AppBarCommand to a value that can be found in the WinJS.UI.AppBarIcon enumeration (see http://msdn.microsoft.com/en-us/library/windows/apps/hh770557.aspx for a full list). For XAML applications, there is a list of common app bar button styles that can be found in the StandardStyles.xaml ResourceDictionary that is included with all XAML application templates in the "Common" folder. Note that the app bar button styles are commented out by default, and you should only uncomment the ones that you need for your app bar.

App Bar Styling Considerations

The app bar is a control that most applications will utilize. For this reason, it is very important for the user experience to be consistent from app to app. Microsoft recommends using the default button styles provided for either XAML or WinJS with regard to placement, size, and padding. The default styles are designed to support up to ten commands in all orientations, on all screen sizes. Changing any of the size-related properties could compromise this design, so this should be avoided. The things you can change are the color of the bar, the color of the buttons, and color of the labels. You should change these to match the branding of your application.

The Right Edge: Charms Bar

One of the most unique aspects of Windows 8 is the Charms bar that is hidden just off the right edge (or left edge, in locales with right-to-left text) of the screen at all times. It houses some very important system-driven functionality that every application can integrate with, including Search, Share, and Settings. The other Charm, Devices, is outside of the scope of this discussion. By checking a few options in your project, and in certain cases, including some additional user-interface pages, you can add abilities to your application that work both in-app and system-wide through the Charms bar. In this section, I'll introduce the following concepts:

- What are Windows 8 app contracts?
- What is a flyout?
- Search charm
- Share charm
- Settings charm

What Are Windows 8 App Contracts?

Before we discuss the individual components of functionality that you can add through the Charms bar, we must explore the concept of app contracts a little bit further. App contracts allow applications to work together, either with each other or with Windows, to complete interesting scenarios or interactions. A contract defines what each participant needs to do to support his or her end of the contract. Each application in the work flow for a particular scenario needs only to worry about implementing its contract.

For example, the Share charm allows users of Windows 8 apps to share content from one application with another application. There are two contracts involved in this interaction: Share Source contract and Share Target contract. The application that wants to share information with other apps on the system will implement the Share Source contract, which simply tells Windows "I have stuff to share with other apps." Other applications on the system that want to share that type of information will implement the Share Target contract and provide some user-interface elements that allow for this sharing to occur. The Share Source and the Share Target applications do not need to know anything about one another. As long as each application successfully implements its contract, Windows 8 will take care of providing the work flow that allows these applications to interact, including presenting the user interface, as needed, and forwarding any relevant information from the source to the target. There are contracts involved in each of the Charms covered in this chapter.

What Is a Flyout?

When a user taps on a charm, a pane slides in from the edge where the Charms bar is located. This type of pane is called a flyout in Windows 8. A flyout used for Charms bar functions takes up the full height of the screen and can be either in a narrow or wide format. The narrow format takes up 346 pixels, and the wide format takes up 646 pixels. A flyout should generally be implemented such that it uses a light dismissal mode. This means that when the user taps on the application somewhere other than where the flyout is located, the flyout should automatically dismiss itself by sliding off the screen. Given this constraint, commands that are placed inside a flyout should automatically commit without the need for such things as "Save" buttons. For example, when using the Settings charm, the options that are presented to the user in the Settings flyout should automatically be applied to the app as the user turns them on and off. This way, the user can feel confident that she can just tap anywhere on the screen to dismiss the flyout.

Some of the Charm functionality can be added to your project through items in the Project's Add ➤ New Item…dialog. In such cases, you will be given a sample flyout to work with. You are also given sample interfaces for both the Share Target and Search contracts when you add them to your project. For the Settings contract, you will have to provide your own flyouts. For JavaScript projects, Microsoft has provided a Settings flyout control that should be used for this purpose. XAML/C# programmers will have to design their own flyout for use with the Settings contract. I will discuss the details of this implementation in the subsection on the Settings contract later in this section.

Search Charm

The Search charm provides users the ability to search the contents of all the applications on the system from anywhere in the operating system. Provided all apps integrate with this capability, users will have a unified search experience across all apps. While Search itself is a fairly basic concept, there are some guidelines you will want to follow to give the users the best Search functionality possible. Providing great search results for compelling content will make users search your application more often—whether they are using your app or someone else's.

Search Is Everywhere

One of the most important things to consider when thinking about the Search charm is whether the interaction it provides is available no matter where the user is in Windows at the time he invokes it. Tapping the Search charm brings out the Search pane from the side of the screen on which the Charms bar is located. Merely typing at this point will search the currently opened app. However, every application that is on the system that is capable of being searched will show up in a list under the Search bar in the pane (see Figure 4-14).

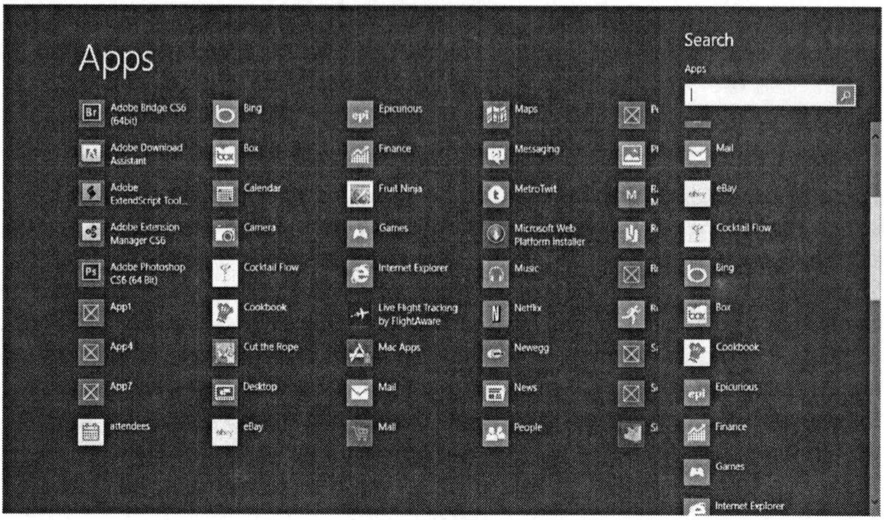

Figure 4-14. Search pane with list of installed applications

Tapping on any of the applications will switch the search results page to the results for the selected application. The applications that are searched the most will move up toward the top of the list over time. This means that no matter where users are and what they are doing, there is a chance that they could use your application when they are searching for something. This makes it especially important to support Search in your application, if you have just about any type of content.

The Search Pane

The first point of contact that users have with the Search interaction is the Search pane. The Search pane has a Search box at the top of the screen and the list of searchable applications at the bottom. When the user begins typing a search query, the application the user is currently using begins to receive the query. When designing for this scenario (the one in which our app is the currently running app), we have two types of suggestions we can provide for the user: query suggestions and result suggestions. Query suggestions are textual suggestions that when tapped will show the search results for that query in the main search results window. A result suggestion is a suggestion that may include an icon or logo, which when tapped, will navigate directly to that item within the application. Note that only five suggestions can be provided in the Search pane, so you should provide only the most relevant results.

Using Query Suggestions

As users type their search queries, an event will be fired that will allow you the opportunity to aid them in their search by offering suggestions. Based on the text the user has entered, you can return some suggestions, providing a shortcut. You should use query suggestions to help users search the content in your application. When a query suggestion is tapped, the search results for the query suggestion should be shown in the application. A query suggestion should always include the text that the user has typed in the Search box. This text can be anywhere within the suggestion that is presented. This is basically a mechanism to provide auto-complete for your search results. For example, if the user has typed "fri," and we have results that include "refrigerator" and "frilly," we would include both of these terms among the query suggestions. The text "fri" in the suggestions should be highlighted in color to indicate that which was matched in providing the particular suggestion. Figure 4-15 shows an example of the Search pane as seen in the Windows Store application providing query suggestions for the term "angry."

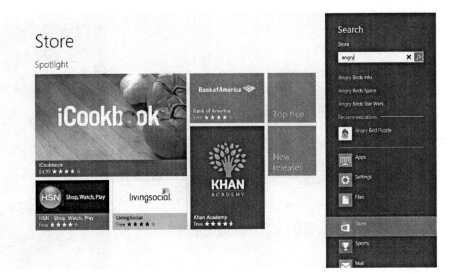

Figure 4-15. Windows Store application query suggestions

Using Result Suggestions

If the text the user has typed into the Search box is sufficient to make a strong suggestion for a particular result in your app's data, you should provide the user with a result suggestion. A result suggestion should provide an icon and a descriptive label to help the user quickly determine whether or not the suggestion is what she is looking for. The main goal of the result suggestion is to allow the user to jump past the usual search results windows and go straight to the result she is looking for. When tapped, the result suggestion will take the user to the details screen for that item within your application. For example, consider Figure 4-16, which illustrates the search "New York ti" in the Windows Store application. The Store application determines there is sufficient information in what the user has typed to confidently suggest "The New York Times" as a result suggestion. The user sees the Times's iconic logo at the beginning of the suggestion and taps on it to download the app. Although not shown in this particular example (although it was illustrated in Figure 4-15), keep in mind that you can show both query and result suggestions in the Search pane.

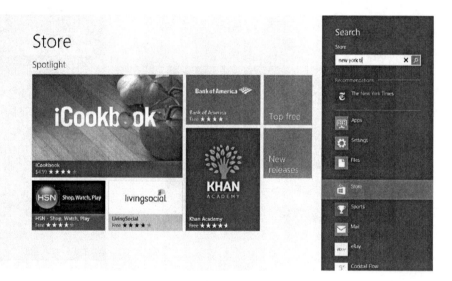

Figure 4-16. Windows Store application result suggestion

Result suggestions work best when you can strongly guess what a user is looking for, based on what they've typed. Consider the application we've explored previously that shows nearby races. If the user is searching for a particular race by name, and he's typed enough of the name to reasonably predict what race he's looking for, a result suggestion should be provided for that race. You can adapt this to your application's data, using a similar strategy.

Search Results

Search would not be all that useful if it only included suggestions in the Search pane. Windows 8 provides a fairly rich search pattern, and this carries through to the search results. Results are typically shown in a format that is consistent with the way items are typically listed in the application that is displaying the results. Usually this implies that the results are shown in a ListView/GridView, depending on the platform. Also fairly commonly included in the search results window is some mechanism for filtering. Figure 4-17 shows the Windows Store application's search results window for the search term "word."

Notice how the search term "word" is clearly called out at the top. The number of results is shown next to the header. Options for changing the sorting and filtering of the results are shown at the top of the results. Finally, the results are shown in a GridView. This is a great example of search results for Windows 8, because it includes enough options to help the user find exactly what he's looking for.

Search Result Ordering

Search results should be ordered such that the most relevant results appear first on the list. The order you choose to show by default largely depends on the nature of your data. The Windows Store results shown in the preceding section (Figure 4-17) are sorted by relevance by default. This probably makes more sense for their data, because they want to present the app they think most closely matches what the typical user would be looking for. If your app deals with time-sensitive material, maybe the default ordering would be based on the specific time the result relates to. Another possibility is to sort the material alphabetically. You will need to analyze your search results on a case-by-case basis to determine a suitable default ordering for your user in that particular scenario and then provide additional options.

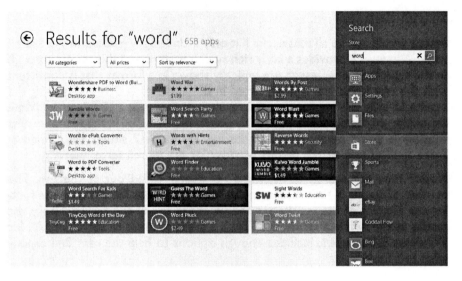

Figure 4-17. Windows Store search results window

In a typical grid layout, results should be ordered from top to bottom and then left to right. If you decide to show your search results in a vertical list, you will want to order them from top to bottom. You should avoid placing very relevant results on the right side of the screen, because the Search pane may still be visible on the screen, if the user has not dismissed it yet.

Best Practices for Displaying Search Results

You should always display the search query that the user typed in order to get to the results. This is important because the Search pane that originated the results will not be visible on the screen once the user has begun to interact with the results. A common format used to display these results places the query in the title area, as shown in the Netflix app in Figure 4-18.

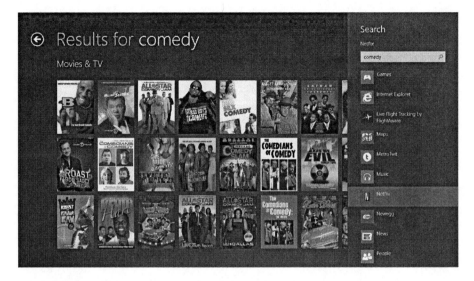

Figure 4-18. Netflix search results prominently display the search term

You should provide a way to scope or filter the results, if that makes sense for your data. For example, the Windows Store search results often span multiple categories and price ranges. Allowing users to specify additional details for their searches from the search results screen will help them find exactly what they are looking for in a more efficient fashion. Figure 4-19 shows the Windows Store application search results for the term "word," with the "Games" category and "Free" price range selected. If you include scoping or filtering, you should consider adding a way to clear the filter to allow the user to easily go back to viewing all results. For example, the filters in the Windows Store application include an "All" option at the top of the filter list. For categories it is "All categories," and for price it is "All prices."

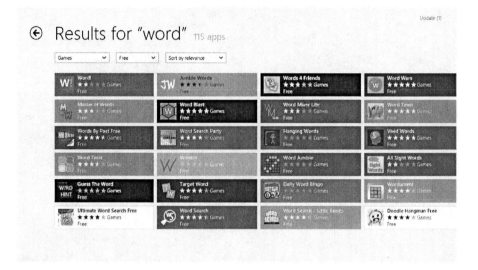

Figure 4-19. Windows Store application search filtering

There are a few other assorted things you should consider adding to your results page. A back button will allow users to easily go back to what they were doing before they invoked a search within your app. Also, if the results you are providing are primarily text-based, you should consider highlighting the search query in the results. This is called "hit highlighting" and helps indicate the relevance of the search query to the results provided. As the query text is updated, code can be written to highlight the relevant text in the results. It's not a good match for all scenarios, but it is something to consider if it makes sense for your search results.

Adding Search to Your Application

Search functionality is so important to the success of Windows 8 applications that Microsoft made it very easy to add it to your project. Whether you are using XAML or HTML/JavaScript, there is a project item that you can add to enable the Search contract. To add the Search contract to your project, right-click on your project and select the Add ➤ New Item . . . option. From the resulting dialog, add the Search contract item. In XAML applications, this will create an XAML page that can be customized and a corresponding code-behind file for handling the Search contract details. In a WinJS application, an HTML page for the search results will be created with a corresponding JavaScript file for handling the Search contract. This is all that is required for a default implementation of Search. You should customize and brand the search results page and add a filtering mechanism, as discussed in the best-practices section. You can provide the query and result suggestions from the code files.

Share Charm

The Share charm is one of the distinguishing features of Windows 8. It has never been so easy for users to share information from one application with another application or service. Windows 8 does a lot of heavy lifting to ease the burden of coordinating the sharing from one app to another by providing the Share Source and Share Target contracts. Apps can participate in either or both sides of the sharing scenario and implement their contract(s). Windows 8 will take care of the rest, as needed, when the user invokes the Share charm.

Always Consider Being a Share Source

Almost every application has features a user might want to share. A news application has articles that a user may want to share on Twitter. A photo-editing application may allow a user to share his photos. A recipe application could allow its users to share a recipe with a friend. A game might allow a user to share her high scores so she can brag to her buddies. The point is, most applications have something in them that people may want to share outside the context of the app from which it originated. Users will come to expect this functionality, as they become familiar with Windows 8. The best apps will provide this option to its users. You can share text (plain or rich), images, URLs, HTML, or developer-defined data schemes. Implementing the Share Source contract is a fairly easy development task, so you should definitely include it among your application design ideas when considering the data in your app.

Share Target Considerations

While the Share Source contract is something most applications should implement, the Share Target should only be considered for applications if they have a valid sharing scenario. The most obvious use for this is for applications that are the front-end for a social network or other "cloud" resource. These applications implement the Share Target as a way to post the shared information to their services. However, this is not the only scenario that can be enabled by using the Share Target. For example, a photo-editing application might implement the Share Target as a way of receiving photos to edit from other applications. One inventive use of the Share Target scenario that can be found in the Windows Store is the Wikipedia application. If you select some text in one application and invoke the Share charm and select Wikipedia, the Wikipedia share target implementation shows Wikipedia results for the selected text (see Figure 4-20).

Figure 4-20. Wikipedia's creative use of the Share Target

Share Target Design

Share Target implementation presents its user-interface components inside a flyout control, as previously discussed in this chapter. The Share flyout typically uses the wide format (646px wide), and this is the format that Visual Studio will take when you add the Share Target to your project. You can still use the narrow format of this if you want, but your Share flyout will be easier to lay out using the wide format. You can add the Share Target to your project by right-clicking the project, then selecting Add ➤ New Item... and choosing "Share Target Contract" from the resulting dialog. This will add the Share Target declaration to your project's app manifest and set it up to receive both text and URL data. If you need to support additional data types, you can add them to the app manifest. Adding the Share Target contract item will also create a flyout for you in either XAML or HTML, depending on the framework you are using to build your application.

By default, the flyout you are provided with will contain a title, a description summary field, a textbox for entering some text, and a "Share" button for triggering the Share operation. The flyout you are provided is intentionally plain. You will want to customize and brand the Share Target experience to match the look and feel of your application. Users of your application should be familiar with the Share experience, if they are frequent users of your application's main interface. For example, compare the main application interface for Tweetro, shown in Figure 4-21, with Tweetro's Share Target flyout, shown in Figure 4-22. Tweetro's designers did a great job of bringing their branded experience over to the Share Target.

Figure 4-21. Tweetro's main interface

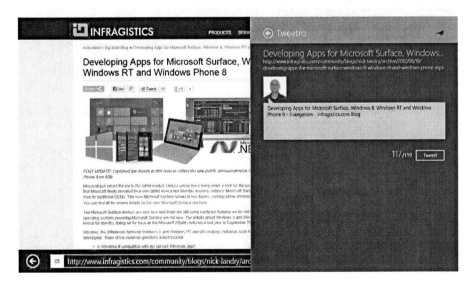

Figure 4-22. Tweetro's Share Target interface

You should keep the interactions in your Share Target interface very simple. Allow users to annotate (comment upon or describe, for example) the things they are sharing, but don't make the work flow too complex. In particular, you should limit the amount of navigation that is necessary in your Share Target interactions and, instead, prefer inline interactions that allow the user to stay on the current page of the flyout. Another thing you can do to make the Share

Target interactions easy to use is to position your "Share" button (the button that says "Tweet!" in Figure 4-22) near the right edge of the screen. This will make the button easy to access with the right thumb. Before dismissing the Share Target flyout, you should indicate to the user that the app is processing the data to be shared. This will give the user confidence that the sharing scenario was successfully achieved.

One other thing you can consider adding to your Share Target implementation is a QuickLink. A QuickLink is a bit like a deep link into your Share Target scenario. For example, consider Mail's Share Target implementation. A user must follow numerous steps to successfully share some content using Mail. First, he must choose an account from which to e-mail. Then, he needs to specify a recipient. Then, he can customize the sharing details and send. In the future, the user might want to e-mail the same person in order to share content. The mail application provides a QuickLink for this specific scenario. This is shown in Figure 4-23, at the top of the list, where it indicates "Email Brent Schooley." Because I'd e-mailed content to myself before, Mail added the QuickLink, so that it becomes easier for me to mail things to myself in the future.

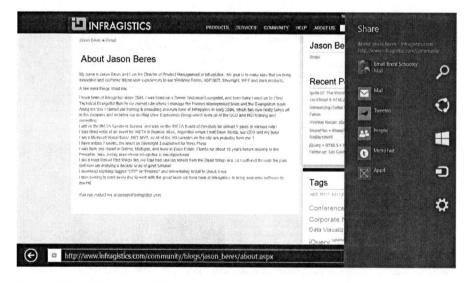

Figure 4-23. Mail adds QuickLinks to ease the sharing process Settings charm

Prior to Windows 8, traditional Windows applications had a problem with consistency when it came to where to place settings. We'd put things in Options under the Tools menu, Settings under the Edit menu, or even Options or Settings under the File menu. How were users to know where to go to edit the application settings? Even more complicated for some users was the Control Panel for system settings. There had long been a need for a consistent location for settings that would be simpler for the average user.

Microsoft recognized this need, and that is what spurred the introduction of the Settings charm. The Settings charm is used for both individual app settings and as the launching point for system-wide settings. The bottom portion of the Settings pane that is launched from the Settings charm houses quick settings for network, brightness, volume, notifications, power, and keyboard. The very bottom of the pane also includes a link that navigates the user to the system settings application. Figure 4-24 shows the bottom portion of the Settings pane. The remaining top portion of the Settings pane is dedicated to the currently running app and is the focus of this section.

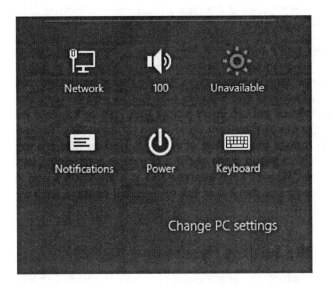

Figure 4-24. The bottom portion of the Settings pane is for system settings

Settings Entry Points on the Settings Pane

The Settings charm experience begins with the Settings pane. Owing to the dual nature of the Settings pane (the top portion is for the app; the bottom is for the system), this pane is provided by the system. While no visual design work is necessary on this pane, you must consider it in your settings design. Your app will provide its settings on a set of flyout controls that you will provide in your application. These flyouts will be launched from entry-point links that are provided on the Settings pane. You should make a list of all the settings you will have in your application and then group them according to similarity (for example, group all of the account-related settings). Give each group a name. These groups will be the entry-point links on the Settings pane. You will want to create as few entry points as necessary. A maximum of four entry points for settings is recommended by Microsoft's design guidelines. By default, all applications get a "Permissions" entry in their Settings pane.

This settings entry informs the user of the application's version number and of any special permissions the app has been granted (such as access to the Internet connection). Windows will also provide a "Rate and review" settings entry point for applications installed through the Windows Store.

In addition to the "Permissions" entry, there is one other settings entry point that should be included in most applications. If your application declares the Internet Connection capability, you will need to include a "Privacy Policy" entry in your Settings pane. Failure to include a privacy policy in your Settings pane in cases where it is required is the most common reason for applications being denied certification. If necessary, make sure to include a "Privacy Policy" entry in your application.

Most settings entry points will launch flyout panes with the corresponding settings for that entry point. However, you may also want to link to the Internet for the Settings pane, in some cases. While this is permitted, you should limit the number of settings entry points that link to web content (for example, to your online privacy policy). Entry points that lead to Internet content should clearly indicate this in their text description by appending "(online)" at the end. One way to reduce the number of external settings that are exposed on the Settings pane is to group them under a common entry point, such as "About." (I have chosen "About" here because this is a common trend in Windows 8 apps as a place to put items that link to external content, such as the creator's web page.)

Designing the Settings Flyout

Once you've defined the entry points for your settings experience, you will need to create a Settings flyout for each entry point. While the implementation details for Settings flyouts differ between WinJS and XAML (I'll briefly discuss those details in the next section), the design goals are the same for each. Settings flyouts can use either the narrow (346px) or wide (646px) format, depending on how much space the settings on the flyout require for clarity. Settings on the flyout should be grouped into sections. Each setting should have a title and a description defining the setting before the control(s) that manipulate the value for the setting. The list of controls that can be used for Settings include

- Toggle switch—used for "on/off" settings
- Button—used to perform immediate actions, such as "Clear history," without dismissing the settings UI
- Hyperlink—takes the user to a different page and closes the settings UI
- Text box—allows the user to specify text, such as a password

- Radio button group—allows the user to select one item from a list of five or fewer options

- Combo box/select—used to allow the user to select one item from a list of six or more options

The controls in the Settings flyout should update immediately, as the user changes them. There is no notion of a "Save" button for the settings, as the settings UI uses a light dismissal mode, like the other charms.

Creating a Settings Flyout in WinJS

As I mentioned earlier in the chapter, the Settings charm is the one charm of the three that have been covered for which no UI is created for the developer by Visual Studio. I'm not exactly sure why a default flyout is not included, but thankfully it is not difficult for us to create one ourselves. Because Visual Studio will not provide a default implementation of the Settings flyout, I figured it would be useful to provide a skeleton implementation for you. Here is a sample flyout in HTML. Note that in WinJS, there is a Settings flyout control in the WinJS.UI namespace for you to use. The "width" property can be set either to wide or narrow.

```
<!doctype HTML>
<html>
    <head>
        <title>Sample Settings Flyout</title>
    </head>
    <body>
        <div data-win-control="WinJS.UI.SettingsFlyout"
            aria-label="Sample settings flyout"
            data-win-options="{settingsCommandId:'sample',width:'wide'}">

            <!-- Background color should match the app's tile background -->
            <!-- Choice of win-ui-dark or light
                depends on text contrast with header -->
            <div class="win-ui-dark win-header"
                style="background-color:#00b2f0">
                <button type="button"
                        onclick="WinJS.UI.SettingsFlyout.show()"
                        class="win-backbutton">
                </button>
                <div class="win-label">Sample</div>
                <img src="../images/smallLogo.png"
                        style="position: absolute; right: 40px;"/>
            </div>
```

```
            <div class="win-content ">
                <div class="win-settings-section">
                        <!-- Settings content goes here -->
                </div>
                <div class="win-settings-section">
                        <!-- May have multiple sections -->
                </div>
            </div>
        </div>
    </body>
</html>
```

The template contains a div with the data-win-control attribute set to WinJS.UI.SettingsFlyout. The first div inside the flyout is the header, which includes a back button, a title label, and a logo, which you can customize. The win-content div contains one or more win-settings-section divs in which you should place your settings for this flyout. If you place this file in /pages/settings/ sample.html, you can load the Settings pane with this flyout using the following code in your default.js file:

```
WinJS.Application.onsettings = function (e) {
    e.detail.applicationcommands =
        { "preferences": { title: "Sample settings flyout", href:
"/pages/settings/sample.html" } };
    WinJS.UI.SettingsFlyout.populateSettings(e);
};
```

Creating a Settings Flyout in XAML

Unlike WinJS, XAML does not provide a Settings flyout control. Instead, we will have to create a page that mimics the same UX guidelines that are used in the WinJS implementation. Here is a sample implementation that you can use as a basis for your Settings flyouts in XAML:

```
<common:LayoutAwarePage
    x:Class="SampleSettingsFlyout"
    xmlns="http://schemas.microsoft.com/winfx/2006/xaml/presentation"
    xmlns:x="http://schemas.microsoft.com/winfx/2006/xaml"
    xmlns:local="using:ApplicationSettings"
    xmlns:common="using:SDKTemplate.Common"
    xmlns:d="http://schemas.microsoft.com/expression/blend/2008"
    xmlns:mc="http://schemas.openxmlformats.org/markup-compatibility/2006"
    mc:Ignorable="d"
    d:DesignHeight="768"
    d:DesignWidth="646">
```

```
<UserControl.Resources>
    <Style x:Key="SettingsBackButtonStyle"
            TargetType="Button">
        <!-- back button style content goes here -->
    </Style>
</UserControl.Resources>

<Border BorderBrush="#00b2f0"
            BorderThickness="1,0,0,0">
    <Grid Background="White"
            VerticalAlignment="Stretch">
        <Grid.RowDefinitions>
            <RowDefinition Height="80"/>
            <RowDefinition Height="*" />
        </Grid.RowDefinitions>

        <!-- Background color should match the app's tile background -->
        <Grid Background="#00b2f0"
                Grid.Row="0">
            <Grid.ColumnDefinitions>
                <ColumnDefinition Width="*" />
            </Grid.ColumnDefinitions>

            <StackPanel x:Name="HeaderPanel" Orientation="Horizontal"
                        Grid.Column="0"
                        Margin="40, 32, 17, 13">
                <Button Click="MySettingsBackClicked"
                        Margin="0,3,0,0"
                        Style="{StaticResource
                                    SettingsBackButtonStyle}"/>
                <TextBlock Margin="10,0,0,0"
                        FontFamily="Segoe UI"
                        FontWeight="SemiLight"
                        FontSize="24.6667"
                        Text="Sample Settings Flyout"
                        Foreground="White"/>
                <Image Source="Assets/smallLogo.png"
                        Margin="400,0,6,0"/>
            </StackPanel>
        </Grid>

        <!-- Settings Panel Content -->
        <ScrollViewer VerticalScrollBarVisibility="Auto"
                Grid.Row="1">
            <Grid Margin="40,33,40,39"
                    VerticalAlignment="Top"
                    Grid.RowSpan="3">
```

```
                <StackPanel x:Name="FlyoutContent">
                    <!-- StackPanel is used to create sections -->
                    <StackPanel>
                            <!-- Settings content goes here -->
                    </StackPanel>

                    <StackPanel Margin="0, 39, 0, 0">
                        <!-- May have multiple sections -->
                    </StackPanel>
                </StackPanel>
            </Grid>
        </ScrollViewer>
    </Grid>
  </Border>
</common:LayoutAwarePage>
```

The StackPanel with x:Name set to "HeaderPanel" contains a back button, a TextBlock for the title, and a logo Image. The StackPanel with x:Name set to "FlyoutContent" can contain multiple sections for the settings on this flyout. On the default page for your application, you will need to handle the CommandsRequested event for the Settings page as follows:

```
SettingsPane.GetForCurrentView().CommandsRequested +=
DefaultPage_CommandsRequested;
```

Our Sample Settings flyout control will have to be hosted within a Popup control that we will configure, so first, we must add a Popup variable to our page, as follows:

```
Popup _settingsPopup;
```

Now, in the CommandsRequested event handler, we will configure the Popup and Sample Settings Flyout and add the Flyout to the Popup, as follows:

```
void DefaultPage_CommandsRequested(SettingsPane sender,
SettingsPaneCommandsRequestedEventArgs args)
        {
            SettingsCommand cmd = new SettingsCommand("sample", "Sample
Settings", (x) =>
                {
                    _settingsPopup = new Popup();
                    _settingsPopup.Closed += OnPopupClosed;
                    Window.Current.Activated += OnWindowActivated;
                    _settingsPopup.IsLightDismissEnabled = true;
                    _settingsPopup.Width = _346;
                    _settingsPopup.Height = _Window.Current.Bounds.Height;
```

```
            var settingsPane = new SampleSettingsFlyout();
            settingsPane.Width = _settingsWidth;
            settingsPane.Height = _windowBounds.Height;

            _settingsPopup.Child = settingsPane;
            _settingsPopup.SetValue(Canvas.LeftProperty,
_Window.Curent.Bounds.Width - _346);
            _settingsPopup.SetValue(Canvas.TopProperty, 0);
            _settingsPopup.IsOpen = true;
        });

    args.Request.ApplicationCommands.Add(cmd);
    }
```

Semantic Zoom

Windows 8 has a strong focus favoring content before chrome. The removal of this chrome results in a flattened application hierarchy. One side effect of this is that, often, the main hub screen will be very long in the horizontal direction. We must provide users with an easy way to jump across this efficiently. This will lead to easier application exploration and traversal. Semantic Zoom enables users with a consistent way to execute this jumping, provided developers and designers include it in their app designs. Semantic Zoom is invoked by pinching inward with two fingers on an application screen. Though there may be some concerns over discoverability with this feature, we can be sure that Microsoft will communicate this feature properly to users if it finds they are not discovering it. So, we should use this feature with confidence and provide our users with this cool new navigation feature.

Basic Semantic Zoom Design

The most basic, fundamental design of Semantic Zoom for a hub-based navigation scheme simply presents the sections as elements that the user can tap on the zoomed-out screen. For example, take a look at the News application's main hub in Figure 4-25 and its Semantic Zoom in Figure 4-26. The sections for the main hub are Top Story, U.S., World, Technology, Politics, Business, Entertainment, and Sports. There is also Advertisement on the end of the hub. All of these sections are represented in the Semantic Zoom view, with a picture that was pulled from one of the stories in the section.

BING DAILY

Figure 4-25. The News application's main hub

Figure 4-26. The News application's Semantic Zoom view

This is the least amount of information that you should provide in your Semantic Zoom view. It allows the user to quickly jump to any of the sections in the News application and gives them a glimpse of what to expect in that section. The News application provides a lot of content, so being able to quickly jump to a section on the end will be very useful to users. This is especially true if they frequently read the Entertainment section. Instead of always having to pan all the way over to the Entertainment section, they can simply invoke Semantic Zoom and tap on it. When they do, they will be taken back to the zoomed-in view, with the application panned over to the section.

Tips for Designing Your Basic Semantic Zoom View

Although its basic concept is fairly simple, there are some things to keep in mind while designing for Semantic Zoom. Try to minimize the need for panning, if you are only providing basic Semantic Zoom functionality. This will maximize the value of the Semantic Zoom for your users. Ideally, you should try to represent all of your sections on one screen, which will require no panning at all. Avoid using only the section name on the Semantic Zoom items. Your goal is for all of the sections to be easily distinguishable from one another at a glance. The News application example offered in the previous section is a great illustration of doing this effectively, by having easily distinguishable imagery and very clear text that relates to the current news for the category.

Implementing Basic Semantic Zoom in WinJS

Adding Semantic Zoom to your application is a fairly simple task. You will need one control that represents the zoomed-in view and one view that represents the zoomed-out view. These controls will have to implement the IZoomableView interface, which basically provides the hooks that make Semantic Zoom work. Thankfully, the ListView control that is used for the majority of hub scenarios implements this interface. The ListView control is the only control provided by WinJS that implements IZoomableView, but it is a very versatile control that is commonly used for hubs. We can create one ListView for the hub and a second ListView for the zoomed-out view. Then, we will wrap those two views with a WinJS.UI.SemanticZoom control, as shown in the following sample:

```
<div data-win-control="WinJS.UI.SemanticZoom">

    <!-- Hub ListView with grouped data -->

    <!-- ListView for zoomed out view which shows the groups -->

</div>
```

The `WinJS.UI.SemanticZoom` control works based on the ordering of the elements added to it. The first view added will be used for the zoomed-in hub, and the second view will be used for the zoomed-out Semantic Zoom view.

The easiest way to achieve this is to first make sure your hub view is working, using your grouped data. Then comment out the hub and get the zoomed out-view working individually with the groups. Then, once you are sure the two views are displaying properly independently, wrap them with the WinJS. UI.SemanticZoom control.

Implementing Basic Semantic Zoom in XAML

Adding Semantic Zoom to your XAML project is similar to adding it to a WinJS project. Just as in the WinJS example, we will create one control for the zoomed-in view and one for the zoomed-out view. XAML provides a SemanticZoom control that takes a ZoomedOutView and a ZoomedInView, much like the WinJS.UI.SemanticZoom control. These both need to be controls that implement IZoomableView. In XAML, there are two controls that implement IZoomableView: ListView and GridView. For SemanticZoom, you will primarily use the GridView control, but keep in mind that the ListView is also an option if a vertical list is preferable for your data. Assuming GridView is used for the hub and zoomed out view, we can write the following code to implement basic Semantic Zoom:

```
<SemanticZoom>

    <SemanticZoom.ZoomedOutView>
        <!-- Hub GridView with grouped data  -->
    </SemanticZoom.ZoomedOutView>

    <SemanticZoom.ZoomedInView>
        <!-- GridView for zoomed out view which shows the groups -->
    </SemanticZoom.ZoomedInView>

</SemanticZoom>
```

Again, you can work on these two views separately, to ensure they are working correctly. Once you feel that both the zoomed-in and zoomed-out views are working correctly independently, you can wrap them with the SemanticZoom control.

Tips for Designing a More Customized Semantic Zoom View

While the basic Semantic Zoom is good for most scenarios, it doesn't really provide much value beyond quick navigation. With such a unique full-screen experience such as Semantic Zoom, it would be a shame not to take advantage of all the screen real estate provided. One of the best ways to take such advantage, is to customize the zoomed-out view to provide more information about the groups. It requires a little bit more thought in the design process to ensure that the group data has sufficient information to customize this view.

For example, imagine if the Bing News application provided a more customized Semantic Zoom experience. One way it could do this would be to show some summary information for each of the News sections. it could elect to show the number of articles for each section, as well as listing when the section was last updated or last read. Adding this information to the Semantic Zoom view would require each section to be able to provide this data, so the designer would have to let the developers know about this design before development began. This is just one example of why it is important to make sure you consider all aspects of your design up front.

For Running Total, I chose to provide a customized Semantic Zoom experience. There is a lot of data in Running Total, and I saw some value in providing yet another way to visualize this data. Semantic Zoom became a great way to customize the data for each individual month and present it in a way that is easy to use. You can see Running Total's Semantic Zoom view in Figure 4-27. It results in a bit more horizontal panning than the basic case, but it is multifunctional, in that it provides another view of the data. One further alteration we have considered for Running Total's Semantic Zoom is to format the months into a column chart, which would make the data even easier to visualize.

Figure 4-27. Running Total's Semantic Zoom view

Summary

In this chapter, I introduced basic app building blocks for Windows 8. For the main content area of the app, I provided some tips to help you design a great grid layout. Then, I walked through the concepts needed to design a great app bar for the bottom of the screen. Following that was a discussion of the three charms you will need to support most of your applications. Finally, I introduced designing for Semantic Zoom. In the next chapter, I will discuss some platform considerations you will need to keep in mind as you design for Windows 8.

Windows 8 Platform Considerations

The Windows 8 platform is very versatile. It offers users the ability to employ touch, keyboard and mouse, and ink for input. The types of machines it runs on range from tablets to laptops to traditional desktops. Apps can run in portrait or landscape orientations across a range of screen sizes and resolutions. The platform even offers a way for two applications to run simultaneously, by snapping one application to the right or left side of the screen. While this versatility is a bonanza for users, when designing apps, it does require that we consider the platform more closely than we might with other operating systems. Therefore, we will concentrate on the following topics in this chapter:

- Designing for touch
- Form factor and layout

Designing for Touch

Windows 8 is not a traditional desktop operating system. It is also not simply a tablet operating system with a "desktop mode." Windows 8 is an operating system that has been designed to be truly touch-first. It runs on many different types of machines, both with and without touch. Because many of these devices have touch, it is imperative that we recognize touch input as a first class citizen on this platform. The good news is that, if we design for touch, we automatically receive support for the mouse and keyboard. There are various components to successfully designing for touch that go beyond merely having objects appear large enough onscreen for a finger to tap. We will have to consider the following:

- The Windows 8 Touch Language
- Touch targets
- Responsiveness
- Task-centered design

The Windows 8 Touch Language

In order to build a touch-first operating system, Microsoft recognized that it needed to define the set of touch interactions that would be supported in the system. Having a consistent set of interactions that it could communicate to developers and users alike was key to the success of the platform. Microsoft captured these interactions into something it calls the Windows 8 Touch Language. This touch language is shown in Figure 5-1.

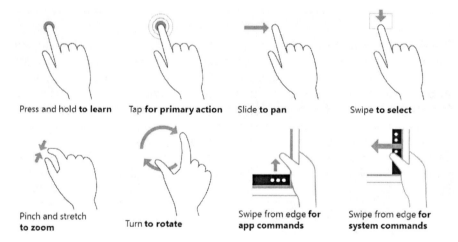

Press and hold **to learn**   Tap **for primary action**   Slide **to pan**   Swipe **to select**

Pinch and stretch **to zoom**   Turn **to rotate**   Swipe from edge **for app commands**   Swipe from edge **for system commands**

Figure 5-1. The Windows 8 Touch Language

These eight simple gestures are the foundation for the touch interactions users will employ to interact with your application and system-wide. It is very important as designers and developers that we do not override these interactions to mean different things. Doing so will only confuse users and make your app undesirable. Instead, you should exploit these gestures knowing that users will be familiar with how they work. Feel free to be creative with the gestures, as long as you do not change their meaning. For example, "pinch and stretch to zoom" can be applied to both optical zoom (such as zooming in on a picture) and Semantic Zoom. The context of the zooming operation is different, but the gesture to perform it is the same.

Many of these interactions will be familiar to most people who have used a tablet or touchscreen phone. For example, the tap, slide, pinch, and rotate gestures have all been used on other platforms to do the same things they do on Windows 8. I do not believe these gestures require further description than that illustrated in Figure 5-1. However, all the other touch interactions have a few elements that warrant consideration when creating your app design.

Press and Hold to Learn

When operating a machine by touch, instead of keyboard and mouse, we lose some interactions we are used to. For example, if I am unsure what a particular toolbar button does in Visual Studio, I know that I can hover my mouse pointer over the button, and a tool tip will appear. This tool tip allows me to ascertain the functionality of that button. Similarly, images in web sites often have tool tips that describe the image in text. When using touch, the user loses the ability to perform a hover interaction, because there is no longer a mouse pointer. Similarly, many applications allow a user to right-click on an element to bring up a context menu with options that can be performed on that item. In a Windows Store application, the app bar is typically used for this type of operation, but what about the desktop that has no app bar?

To enable mouse interactions in touch, Microsoft chose to use the "press and hold to learn" gesture. If you want to provide tool tips for elements in your Windows Store applications, they will be visible on elements if the user presses and holds on the element. The "press and hold" gesture can also be used to trigger context menus, where appropriate. The primary location where this will be used is on the desktop, because right-clicking will not be an option using touch. The most important thing to note about "tap and hold" is that it should only be used for this type of "additional information" behavior. On other platforms, "tap and hold" has been used to enter "modes," such as reordering of icons. Do not use "tap and hold" for this type of behavior. Instead, you should allow the user to simply drag to reorder directly, without having to enter a mode. This is how reordering is done on the Start screen.

Swipe to Select

Another new gesture in the Windows 8 arsenal is "swipe to select." On some other platforms, you must enter an "edit mode" in order to operate on the items in a list. This requires users to enter a different context than the one they are currently in, only for the purposes of performing actions on items.

For example, in order to share pictures from the Photos application on iOS, a user must tap on a button to enter a mode where she is able to select photos. After activating the edit mode, tapping on a photo will select it, instead of opening it. Basically, the same gesture is used on the same item on the same screen to mean two completely different things. To avoid this overloading, and also to avoid the "entering a mode" phenomenon, Microsoft chose to implement selection differently on Windows 8 than on other platforms.

One of Microsoft's guiding principles in the design of its touch interactions is to let fingers do what they are good at. From an ergonomic perspective, swiping down slightly on an item is a very natural gesture that is easy for the hands to perform. However, it is not a gesture that is commonly used for anything on touch platforms. Given the fact that the standard orientation for most applications on Windows 8 is landscape, this implies that most applications will pan horizontally to browse content. This frees the natural swipe down on an item as a potentially useful gesture. Microsoft chose to take advantage of this as a mechanism to select items in a list. A gentle downward swipe on an item in a grid view that enables selection will select the element. When items are selected, the app bar will appear on the bottom of the screen to enable contextual commands based on selection (see Figure 5-2). Selecting more elements in the list is as simple as swiping on more elements. Incidentally, you don't have to "enter a mode" to move items around in a list that allows reordering. All you have to do is move the item!

Figure 5-2. "Swipe to select" enables contextual behaviors

The implications on your app design based on the existence of "swipe to select" are fairly simple. Obviously, as stated several times before, do not override this gesture to provide some other functionality. More particularly, however, you should also not require your users to "enter a mode" in order to delete, rename, or perform actions on the elements in a list. You should simply enable selection on your list and use the app bar to provide this contextual functionality. Users will come to expect this behavior, as they use more and more apps in Windows 8.

Swipe from the Bottom Edge for App Commands

Windows 8 applications by their nature are intended to dedicate the entire screen to the content of the application. This means that a majority of the commands we would typically place into toolbars or as buttons directly on the app canvas need a place to live. As discussed in the Chapter 4, the place for the majority of these commands is the app bar at the bottom of the screen. I included this gesture in the list of gestures to discuss in this section simply because I wanted to acknowledge the difference between how the gesture works and its mouse equivalent. To invoke the app bar on a keyboard-and-mouse setup, the user can right-click anywhere on the application. This interaction is the same as selecting an item with keyboard and mouse. I believe this is an area where touch has a distinct advantage. The mouse interaction is somewhat overloaded, but the touch gesture is unique. I don't have to stress again the "don't overload this gesture" mantra, because you cannot, in fact, override this gesture—the system owns it!

Swipe from the Left, Right, and Top Edges for System Commands

Similar to the "swipe from bottom" gesture, swiping from the left and right edges is reserved by the system. In this case, rather than providing users with commands for your application, the edges are for system functionality. Swiping from the left edge enables the user to switch between recently opened applications. Swiping from the right edge enables the Charms bar. Swiping entirely from top to bottom closes the currently running app. Swiping down from the top but then moving to the right or left side of the screen enables the user to "snap" the application to that side of the screen (more on snapping later in this chapter). When combined with the previous section's "swipe from bottom" gesture, we can quickly realize that Windows 8 owns all of the edges! In fact, the single pixel border around the edge of your application is the only set of pixels that Windows 8 claims for its own. What this means for you as a designer is that you should not attempt to get clever and use your own edge. These are reserved for use by the system, and users will be expecting them to work the way the system intends.

Touch Targets

Any discussion regarding a touch-driven system would be incomplete without mentioning touch target sizes. Touch target size refers to the area that can be tapped in order to activate an onscreen element. This does not necessarily have to be exactly the same size as the "visible" portion of the element. For example, a circular button might visually occupy an onscreen area that is too small to reliably tap. In this case, the developer might choose to make the tappable area for this button larger than the onscreen circle. The touch target for this button would be the tappable area, not what is seen on screen.

What size is best for touch targets? The truth is, there is no such thing as a "best size," as this would imply there is a size that eliminates mistakes and does not completely monopolize your app's screen real estate. Usability studies have shown that even with relatively large touch targets, users still make mistakes. The number of mistakes may decrease, but they cannot be eliminated. Therefore, it is important to consider different touch target sizes for different scenarios.

The average minimum touch target size that works for most scenarios is 7x7mm. Note that the touch target is described in physical dimensions, not pixels. This is because screens have different densities, and 10 pixels on one screen can be vastly smaller or bigger than on another. It is important, then, to describe touch targets with respect to how large they are on the physical device. Provided an action can be reversed by one or two gestures, the 7x7mm minimum touch target size will work fine. Touch targets smaller than this may cause frustration. Note, too, that you will want at least 2mm padding between each target. This padding contributes almost as much to the reduction of touch errors as the size itself!

To prevent an action that could potentially result in irreversible consequences (such as "delete"), you will want to use a slightly larger than average touch target. This will reduce the potential for errors. The Windows 8 touch interaction guidelines suggest a minimum target size of 9x9mm for this type of touch target. On average, a touch target of 9x9mm reduces the amount of errors in half, compared to a touch target of 7x7mm. Given the circumstances, you will be doing your users a favor by bumping up the size of your targets for these scenarios. As with the 7x7mm targets, remember to keep a minimum of 2mm padding between targets, to further reduce the occurrence of accidental taps.

There are almost certainly going to be occasions when you will have to fit just a little bit more than usual into certain areas of the screen. That is okay, as long as what you are trying to jam together is used infrequently. As long as the actions performed by these smaller touch targets can be reversed using a single gesture, it is okay to use touch targets as small as 5x5mm. You will want to carefully examine any instance in which you use targets that are this small, to ensure that they are not being used for a frequent interaction. Note that with the smaller target size, the padding becomes extremely important. Padding of 2mm is still recommended, but in this case, it represents almost half of the target size. Having this padding on both sides of a small target will be almost essential to its success.

Responsiveness

Touch devices differ from mouse-and-keyboard systems in some very interesting respects. Some of the differences have to do with user psychology. Without delving too deeply into the emotions informing such differences (since I'm not an expert on the subject), it is known that users react differently to directly manipulating an onscreen item via touch than they do to interacting with elements using a mouse pointer. This has something to do with the fact that all throughout our lives, we interact with things by touch. We have grown accustomed to what is called "direct manipulation." Direct manipulation means simply touching an element directly to operate it. To move a cup from a counter to a sink, for example, we pick it up with our hand and move it to the sink. The mouse-and-keyboard equivalent of this action would necessitate explaining to a friend how to get the cup, commanding him to pick up the cup, navigating him to the sink, and telling him to drop the cup. The same task is accomplished following this scenario, but there is a level of indirection involved. If our friend has difficulty picking up the cup, we feel some measure of frustration, but it is mitigated by the fact that we don't experience the sensation of picking up the cup ourselves.

This analogy holds true as we come back to the technology world. We are more likely to experience frustration when we interact directly with elements on the screen and things do not immediately respond. Imagine if you pushed a button on your keyboard, and the letter took five seconds to appear on the screen. You would quickly become frustrated with the keyboard. The same is true when you tap an onscreen button. If there is no immediate indication on screen of a successful tap interaction, a user may quickly become frustrated with your application. In fact, the user will probably continue to tap an element in this situation, and in some apps, this will cause problems, due ultimately to performing the action multiple times. It is extremely important to provide some level of immediate feedback (primarily visual, but you can explore auditory feedback as well) when a user interacts with elements in your application.

Another example of providing proper feedback for touch is when the user performs an operation to move onscreen elements. The content should "stick to" the user's finger as she moves the element. This provides the user with constant validation that the element is actually being moved where it is being directed. Imagine you were moving a sheet of paper on your desk, but it lagged several inches behind you. This occurrence would be even worse if the paper didn't actually move until you put your hand (holding an abstract representation of it) in the desired location. It seems silly, but both of these scenarios have played out in the past for mouse interactions involving moving items. The key point here is that it would be just as silly to do with onscreen elements what is done in the real world with paper, so make sure elements being moved stick to the user's finger throughout the move operation.

Users do not need fireworks to explode to indicate that they have successfully initiated an operation. A simple shrinking of an element that is currently being pressed can indicate that the item is "pressed down." The element can briefly highlight after being successfully tapped to indicate completion of the action before continuing. You should provide some sort of indication of progress, if the resulting operation is going to take longer than a few seconds. For indeterminate lengths of time, you should show a progress ring near the point of interaction or an indeterminate progress bar at the top of the screen. If you know how long the operation is going to take or if it can be broken down into percentages, you should consider showing a progress bar indicating this information. Basically, you should strive to keep the user informed that something is happening in response to their action. Our applications should do this regardless of touch or mouse interaction, but it is especially important in touch scenarios, so that users do not feel as if they have done something wrong.

Task-Centered Design

For applications on touch devices, such as tablets, to be successful, they have to help users accomplish tasks quickly and efficiently. Complex work flows with abstract representations of concepts simply will not work in this context. Because users on touch-based systems are very likely to want to get things accomplished and move on to the next thing, we must design methodology that helps to deliver an experience that maps well to what the user has set out to do with your app. Thankfully, there is a design methodology that fits the bill for this purpose. It also combines well with the "best at" statement concepts we discussed in previous chapters. The methodology we'll explore for realizing our design is called task-centered design.

Task-centered design is a usability design methodology that emphasizes creating an interface that supports a user in the process of completing a specific task. An application that is designed using task-centered goals will guide a user through the task, asking for pertinent information only when it is required. Users will never be presented with tools or information that does not completely support accomplishing a specific task. The flow through the application's screens should closely match the user's mental workflow for completing the task.

A big benefit of task-centered design is that it leads to much more intuitive and easy-to-use software. If the software is truly designed to match the task at hand, the users will have a greater level of confidence when availing themselves of the application. They will feel they are less prone to making mistakes. Users will feel a sense of accomplishment and that the app is truly beneficial. This is exactly what we are aiming to provide in a touch-based experience. The "best at" statement and scenarios that we created for our applications in Chapter 3 are a great starting point for task-centered design. Take the scenarios and focus on them as tasks. Constantly make sure that what you are presenting on each screen is exactly what the user needs—no more, no less.

Form Factor and Layout

One of the most interesting and challenging aspects of Windows 8 from a design perspective is the variety of different screen sizes, resolutions, densities, and form factors that the operating system can run on. For tablets and some desktop monitors, we must support both a landscape and portrait viewing mode. An app can have four modes of layout: landscape, portrait, snapped, and fill. On screens with a pixel width greater than 1366, the user is able to "snap" an application to the right or left side of the screen. In this snapped view mode, the application will take up 320 pixels. The remainder of the screen can be taken up by another application, which runs in what is called "fill" mode. In addition to the layout modes, we also have to consider different screen sizes and densities. These have a big impact on the placement of elements and the quality of the design assets that are needed in the application. The topics that will be covered in this section are

- Landscape vs. portrait

- Snapped and fill views

- Designing for different screen sizes

- Designing for different screen densities

Landscape vs. Portrait

Most computer monitors and laptop screens today have either 16:10 or 16:9 aspect ratios. In other words, they are wider than they are tall. This means that when designing a full-screen experience, the default orientation for these screens would be landscape. Microsoft decided to embrace this aspect ratio when designing Windows 8 for tablets as well. The default resolution for Windows 8 tablets is 1366x768. Tablets built with this aspect ratio will be considerably wider in one direction than in the other. This means that for these screens the default orientation is landscape as well. Windows 8 was designed with this "landscape first" mentality in mind. By default, the Start screen is a horizontally panning list of tiles (shown in Figure 5-3). In 1366x768 resolution, there are three rows of tiles that span as far to the right as needed.

Figure 5-3. The Start screen in landscape format pans horizontally

However, tablets and some computer monitors can be rotated into a portrait orientation. Windows 8 supports the portrait orientation, and tablets will autorotate to this orientation as needed. This means that applications will have to support portrait orientation as well. The Windows 8 Start screen adjusts its content when in portrait mode. As shown in Figure 5-4, the Start screen adjusts to show six rows instead of the three rows it displayed in landscape. Note that the panning direction on the Start screen is still horizontal. The designers of the screen simply decided to take up more space in the vertical direction.

Figure 5-4. In portrait orientation, the Start screen shows more rows

There are a lot of guidelines and examples that show how to design for land-scape, as it is the default orientation for Windows 8. There are not nearly as many examples on what to do to support portrait mode. As there seems to be a lack of guidance in this area, I will spend the bulk of this section talking about portrait. The portrait orientation has some definite strengths and weaknesses that you will need to consider when designing your app's portrait view modes. Landscape will be the preferred orientation for most users in most applications, but there are some definite strong cases for portrait.

Portrait Is Great for Reading

With its longer-than-wide form factor, the portrait orientation is a natural fit for reading. Most print formats are in a similar form factor, so we are accustomed to reading this way. The reason for this is that we have a much easier time reading text in columns that are not too wide. In landscape, we have to break the text up into columns, in order to read text effectively. This is similar to what newspapers have to do to make text readable. In portrait, we have the ability to lay out our text in a single column. For many users, this will provide a much better reading experience, because it more closely resembles the format they are used to from reading books. For example, compare the landscape orientation of the Bing News app shown in Figure 5-5 to the portrait orientation in Figure 5-6 of the same article. Note: The image is still available with the article, it's just no longer in flow on the same page. It's "below the fold."

Figure 5-5. A iBing News article shown in landscape orientation

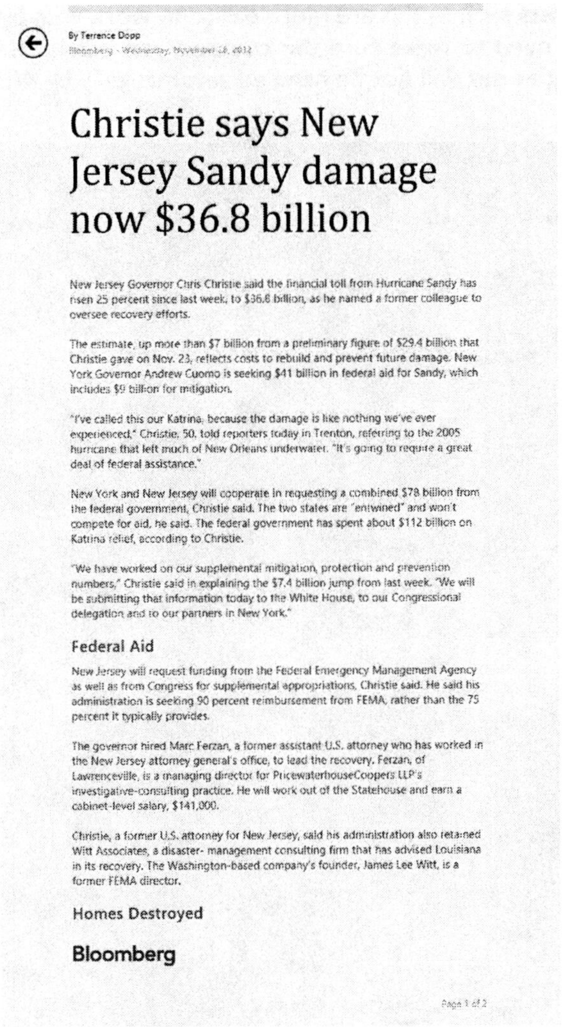

By Terrence Dopp

Bloomberg - Wednesday, November 28, 2012

Christie says New Jersey Sandy damage now $36.8 billion

New Jersey Governor Chris Christie said the financial toll from Hurricane Sandy has risen 25 percent since last week, to $36.8 billion, as he named a former colleague to oversee recovery efforts.

The estimate, up more than $7 billion from a preliminary figure of $29.4 billion that Christie gave on Nov. 23, reflects costs to rebuild and prevent future damage. New York Governor Andrew Cuomo is seeking $41 billion in federal aid for Sandy, which includes $9 billion for mitigation.

"I've called this our Katrina, because the damage is like nothing we've ever experienced," Christie, 50, told reporters today in Trenton, referring to the 2005 hurricane that left much of New Orleans underwater. "It's going to require a great deal of federal assistance."

New York and New Jersey will cooperate in requesting a combined $78 billion from the federal government, Christie said. The two states are "entwined" and won't compete for aid, he said. The federal government has spent about $112 billion on Katrina relief, according to Christie.

"We have worked on our supplemental mitigation, protection and prevention numbers," Christie said in explaining the $7.4 billion jump from last week. "We will be submitting that information today to the White House, to our Congressional delegation and to our partners in New York."

Federal Aid

New Jersey will request funding from the Federal Emergency Management Agency as well as from Congress for supplemental appropriations, Christie said. He said his administration is seeking 90 percent reimbursement from FEMA, rather than the 75 percent it typically provides.

The governor hired Marc Ferzan, a former assistant U.S. attorney who has worked in the New Jersey attorney general's office, to lead the recovery. Ferzan, of Lawrenceville, is a managing director for PricewaterhouseCoopers LLP's investigative-consulting practice. He will work out of the Statehouse and earn a cabinet-level salary, $141,000.

Christie, a former U.S. attorney for New Jersey, said his administration also retained Witt Associates, a disaster- management consulting firm that has advised Louisiana in its recovery. The Washington-based company's founder, James Lee Witt, is a former FEMA director.

Homes Destroyed

Bloomberg

Page 1 of 2

Figure 5-6. The same Bing News article shown in portrait orientation

Portrait Is Great for Lists

Reading is not the only beneficiary of the vertical nature of portrait orientation. Data that is best represented in list form also looks great in portrait. The application in the Windows Store that has done the best job so far in displaying this type of data in portrait is Tweetro. Tweetro is a Twitter client for Windows 8. When displaying a time line in portrait mode, Tweetro reflows the list so that it spans the length of the screen vertically (see Figure 5-7). For this mode, Tweetro also switches the panning direction from horizontal to

vertical. Long lists such as this are much easier to work with by panning vertically. You will need to make sure the controls you use in the portrait view
scroll vertically, as this will not be handled automatically by Windows.

Figure 5-7. Tweetro takes advantage of the vertical viewport in portrait

Do What Is Best for Your Content

The most important thing to do when designing the portrait mode for your
application is to really think about the content you are displaying on a particular screen. In some cases, such as the main hub, you may want to keep the

same format as in landscape. You may also want to keep the horizontal panning from the landscape view when you move to portrait. However, if the content warrants it, you may want to reflow the content so that it takes advantage of the additional vertical space. This is especially useful for content that is intended to be read or data that can be displayed in list form, as previously discussed. Whatever you do, however, do not neglect the portrait orientation. Though most users will use your application in landscape, there will be those who prefer to use their devices in portrait. You must be sure to provide these users with a good experience.

Snapped and Fill Views

Some touch-based operating systems only allow one application at a time. Windows 8 allows two applications to run on the screen. This mode is known as "snapping" in Windows 8. The user can perform a gesture (drag down from the top and then over to the right or the left) or a key combination to move one application to the right or left side of the screen. The snapped application takes up the full height of the screen at 320 pixels wide. The other application on the screen fills up the remaining portion in a view state known as "fill." This is a very unique approach for multitasking, and both snapped and fill modes require some design attention to ensure that you provide the best experience for users of your design.

Designing Your Snapped View

When your application is snapped by the user to the left or right side of the screen, it is resized to have a width of 320 pixels. It is important to note that nothing should change in your app in terms of functionality when moving from a full-width view to the snapped view. You should always strive for feature parity between your snapped and normal views. You will, however, need to change the way your screens are laid out. If the content in your full-screen application does not fit on a single screen, it will lay out its content such that panning horizontally reveals more content. When your application is snapped, it becomes much taller than it is wide. In fact, one way to consider the snapped view in terms of design is to think of it as a tall phone-sized view. You have to think about designing your app as if it were a phone application.

In concrete terms, your application will transition from a view where horizontal panning is appropriate to one where it makes much more sense to use vertical panning. Your hub views will need to change to a vertically panning list. You should use a similar design style for the different views, but you may need to make the content more compact to fit the width. For example, Running Total's hub view when snapped (shown in Figure 5-8) still has the street background and blue tile styling. However, instead of a horizontally panning hub, it is now a vertical list. Tapping a tile or section header still navigates to the item or section details screen, just as it would in the full-screen view.

Figure 5-8. Running Total's hub view in snapped mode

You may also need to change the way your data is presented onscreen when in snapped mode. You still want to present the same content, but the form factor difference may force you to approach it differently. For example, Running Total's section details screen shows the total for each day of the month in a column chart when in full-width mode. This style of data presentation would be completely unreadable, let alone easy to tap, in the snapped view. To circumvent this issue but still show the same data, Running Total switches from a column chart to a bar chart when it is snapped, as shown in Figure 5-9.

Figure 5-9. Running Total's section details view in snapped mode

Taking a view that normally takes up a minimum of 1024 pixels and figuring out how to make it work in a width of 320 pixels can be very challenging. In some cases, you will have to figure out very different ways to present the same information that is available in the full-width view. The most important thing to keep in mind is to bring the same functionality to your snapped view as you do to your full-screen view. Your snapped view is not a widget, or minimized version, of your app. It is simply a resized version of it. Remember to maintain application state as you move in and out of snapped view, as you would with any other screen transition in a Windows Store app. Users will expect to have a continuous experience, as they switch views.

Special Considerations for Fill View

Fill view is essentially your normal view minus 342 pixels (the snapped view plus the 22 pixel splitter). This means that, in most cases, you will not have to do anything in order to support the fill view, because Windows will resize the app for you. The horizontal panning that you have in your normal view will still work well in the fill view. There are a few cases where not being full-screen may require you to modify your layout for the fill view. One case where you may need to make a change when you enter fill mode is when you have controls that have been optimized for screen-edge usage. If your app has controls on the right and left edge that are intended to be manipulated by the user's thumbs simultaneously, this will not work in fill view. One of the two edges will be difficult to reach, due to the snapped app. In this type of scenario, it will be useful to reposition these controls so that the user will realize the previous way of working with the app has been modified in this new view. One pos-sible solution to this is to move all of these buttons to one side of the screen (either right, left, top, or bottom). You may also consider combining buttons, if possible, so that one button makes multiple functions available.

The other case in which you might need to make a layout change in fill view is when your content has been designed for a fixed size and you do not want to use scaling to shrink it. For example, an application that has a screen with a precisely sized three-column layout at 1366 pixels wide will not have sufficient room when shown at 1024 pixels in fill view. This app will need to make a change. If scaling is not an option, one of the columns should be omitted from the fill view. In this scenario, it is a good idea to find another way to allow the user to access the hidden content.

Designing for Different Screen Sizes

As mentioned previously, Windows 8 can run on a variety of different types of machines with a variety of different screen sizes. These screen sizes range from 10.6-inch tablet-sized screens to 27-inch and larger screens for desk-tops, all the way up to crazy 82-inch touchscreen TV monitors. Each screen size introduces more screen real estate for your application to take up, and you will need to have a strategy for having your app occupy that space when it is available. For a minimum size, you should plan on 1024x768. This is the low-est pure resolution allowed by Windows 8, and it is also the lowest resolution for an application in fill view. You should also plan for an optimal minimum resolution of 1366x768, because this is the smallest resolution that supports snapped and fill views. When dealing with larger screen sizes, you will need to fill the additional space with your application. There are two major techniques for doing this: fixed layout and adaptive layout.

Fixed Layout for Larger Screens

One strategy for dealing with different sizes of screens is to keep the same layout, scaling it up or down, depending on the size of the screen. The Windows 8 design guidelines refer to this as a "fixed layout." In the web design world, a fixed layout means that elements will not scale. In Windows, this is not the case. A fixed layout means everything is explicitly placed for one resolution and then scales up to other resolutions. This is a very effective strategy for games. In a game, the introduction of more screen real estate typically does not add any value, because the player still wants to have the same game experience. For example, the game Cut the Rope has exactly the same play experience at 10.6 inches (shown in Figure 5-10) as it does at 27 inches. The game's creators have simply scaled the view to the size needed.

Figure 5-10. Cut the Rope scales, as needed, for larger screens

The most important thing you need to bear in mind when you scale a fixed layout is that your images will scale as well. You will need either to provide vector graphics or higher resolution bitmaps. If you provide higher resolution bitmaps, you will want to provide images that are twice the size of the ones you would need for the design size. It is much better for your images to require scaling down than scaling up. Your initial layouts should begin with 1024x768 and 1366x768. These are the layouts that will be scaled up to larger screen sizes. Another thing to keep in mind is that if the scaled layout does not precisely fit the aspect ratio of the new screen, it will be centered and let-terboxed. The letterbox will be the color of the application's background, so you will want to choose that background color to match your application.

Adaptive Layout for Larger Screens

The other strategy for dealing with larger screen sizes is to adapt your lay-out. By this technique, some or all of your layout takes up more space on the screen, while other parts stay at a fixed size and location. For example, many applications will have header and footer regions that will have a fixed size and a content region that stretches to take up the remaining size. You will want to define the regions of your application that need to stretch and the directions they will stretch in. If you have a GridView/ListView in the main content area of your hub, you will probably want to set this to stretch in both directions, to accommodate as many items as will fit on a larger screen.

For Running Total, the dashboard summary section of the hub on the far-left side of the application has a fixed width, but it can scale vertically as needed.

The remaining area of the app is filled with more tiles in the vertical direction, as needed, due to setting the GridView to stretch in both the vertical and horizontal directions. The header text with the name of the app stays fixed at the top, regardless of screen size. Running Total at 10.6 inches is shown in Figure 5-11 and at 27inches in Figure 5-12.

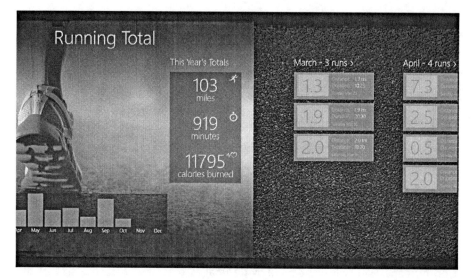

Figure 5-11. Running Total on a 10.6-inch, 1366x768 screen

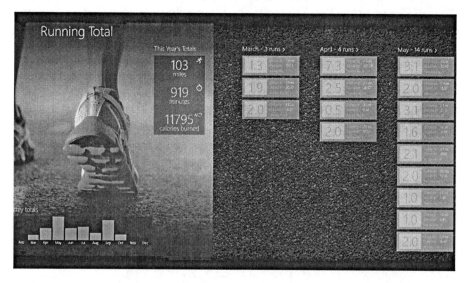

Figure 5-12. Running Total on a 27-inch, 2560x1440 screen

For your application, you will want to determine exactly how you plan to occupy the extra screen space. You can elect to show more information, or you can choose to show the same amount of information by increasing the degree of white space in the design. Ultimately, no matter what you decide to do, the key is to make sure the experience is great, no matter what the screen size is.

Designing for Different Screen Densities

Screen size is not the only factor that we need to keep in mind as we discuss the various screens Windows 8 can run on. Screen technology has been increasing at a rapid rate in the past few years, and manufacturers now have access to screens with a much higher pixel density than in years past. This can lead to dramatically clearer text and image quality, which, in turn, provides a much better experience for users. However, as the pixel density of a screen increases, the physical objects on screen get smaller. At some point, the items on screen become too small for the user to read.

Windows 8 automatically scales the entire operating system, including both the system and application user interface, at various densities. This scaling can accord to one of three different scaling percentages, based on the pixel density of the screen. The scale percentage will be 100 percent when there is no scaling applied. On devices with a resolution of 1920x1080 with a minimum DPI (dots per inch) of 174, Windows 8 will change the scale percentage to 140 percent. The scale percentage will increase to 180 percent on devices with a resolution of 2560x1440 and a minimum DPI of 240. Nothing is required of you to request scaling for your application; however, you will have to consider the effects of image scaling (such as blur or pixelation) on your app design.

Consider Using Vector Graphics

Every image in your application will be scaled when your app UI is scaled at increased DPI. If your application uses vector graphics, images will stretch and scale without any loss in quality, due to how vector graphics are drawn. If you are using WinJS, you can provide your vector graphics using SVG. For XAML applications, you can specify your vector graphics using XAML. Windows will automatically scale both of these types of vector graphics for you, with no noticeable degradation in quality.

Provide Scaled Bitmaps, If Necessary

Sometimes you will be unable to use vector graphics in your application. In such cases, it is important to provide bitmaps that look good at each of the scale percentages. This means you will have to provide one bitmap for

100 percent, one for 140 percent, and another for 180 percent. There are two naming conventions for specifying how Windows should determine which bitmap to use at runtime: file naming convention and folder naming convention.

For the file naming convention, you will add scale-100, scale-140, or scale-180 between the file name and the extension for each bitmap. For example, for an image named shoe.jpg, the corresponding file names for the different scale percentages would be the following (assuming you have an images folder at the root of the project):

```
/images/shoe.scale-100.jpg
/images/shoe.scale-140.jpg
/images/shoe.scale-180.jpg
```

For the folder naming convention, you will place each version inside a folder that contains the scale in the folder name. For example, for an image named shoe.jpg, the corresponding file names for the different scale percentages would be as follows (again assuming an images folder at the root of the project):

```
/images/scale-100/shoe.jpg
/images/scale-140/shoe.jpg
/images/scale-180/shoe.jpg
```

When specifying the file name in HTML or XAML, you will simply provide the file name without the naming convention. Windows will find the right image to use, depending on the scale percentage currently in use by the system. To avoid shifts in layout when larger images are loaded, make sure to specify widths and heights on your images, instead of relying on autosizing. For example, if you have an image that is 100px wide by 300px high, you should specify these height and width values on the image control in your markup. If you are manually loading images at runtime, or fetching images from the Web, you must make sure you are getting the correctly sized image for the current DPI setting. Use the appropriate CSS media queries or WinRT APIs to select the best image for the current situation.

Work Within the Typographic Grid Units

We discussed the Windows 8 typographic grid in the first few chapters of this book. When discussing scaling, this concept becomes especially important. It is essential for your app UI to align to either the 5 pixel subunits or the 20 pixel major units of the typographic grid. Any elements that do not align to multiples of 5 pixels may be subject to pixel shifting, due to pixel rounding. The end result of this is a potentially blurry application. You should aim to avoid this in your application.

Summary

In this chapter, you were introduced to certain elements you must consider with regard to the Windows 8 platform. The two major areas of focus were designing for touch and dealing with various form factors and layout. The Windows 8 Touch Language, touch target sizes, and responsiveness were all discussed. Then a brief look was taken at task-centered design and how it can help in building touch-first designs. For form factor, the implications of portrait, snapped, and fill view modes on app layout were touched on. Some strategies for dealing with various screen sizes and pixel densities were also explored. In Chapter 6, I will discuss some strategies for converting your existing application designs to Windows 8.

Bringing Existing Apps to Windows 8

Since Windows 8 was announced, I have been studying it, blogging about it, and giving presentations related to it. Throughout this process, there has been one question that I get asked repeatedly: "Windows 8 looks great ... but how do I bring my existing application to it?" This is a perfectly valid question. Not every application for Windows 8 is a brand-new application. Many applications released on Windows 8 already exist on one or more other platforms. In almost all of these cases, the application in question will need to undergo a bit of a transformation before landing in the Windows Store. In a process Microsoft calls "reimagining," apps must shed the UI patterns (or lack thereof, in some cases) of their current platform in order to fit into the Windows 8 ecosystem. In this chapter, I will explain the process involved in transforming a traditional Windows desktop application into a Windows Store application. I will then discuss a few strategies you can employ to bring tablet applications from other platforms onto Windows 8. In many ways, this chapter is a culmination of everything you have learned so far in this book. For each stage of the transformation, I will refer to the underlying reasons for each change. Many things will relate back to the design principles you learned in Chapter 2.

From Desktop to Windows Store

Traditional Windows desktop applications require a lot of thought and effort to successfully transfer to Windows 8. For starters, a majority of Windows desktop applications were not designed with touch in mind. In fact, many of these applications' original versions were developed before touchscreens were mainstream. The older versions of Windows used to develop them were not created with touch as a primary focus. These "classic" applications were developed with keyboard and mouse as the main input source, and it shows. Small toolbar buttons that would be next to impossible to tap with a finger of any reasonable size are everywhere on these applications. Touch target size issues are not only limited to toolbars, though. Most elements on classic desktop applications are too small to reliably tap.

Even though the touch target size issue is a major one, there are many more significant hurdles to overcome for classic desktop applications on their way to becoming Windows Store apps. As I have discussed throughout the book, one of the driving forces of the Microsoft design language is the favoring of content over chrome. One of the principal shortcomings of traditional desktop applications in relation to these ideals is an overemphasis on chrome. As you will see from the application, to which we will apply a Windows Store makeover, some applications spend a lot of their features and screen real estate on elements that are tangential to the app's main purpose. We will have to find the proper place for each of these non-content features within the Windows 8 infrastructure and focus the application on its intended purpose. Remember that at the end of the process, you want to have an application that is truly great at helping a user accomplish a specific task or goal. You want it to be the "best at" something.

Target Application: RSS Reader

The application we will transform from a classic desktop application to a Windows Store app is a traditional RSS Reader application. Shown in Figure 6-1, this application is supposed to be great at enabling users to keep up to date on articles and feeds they want to read.

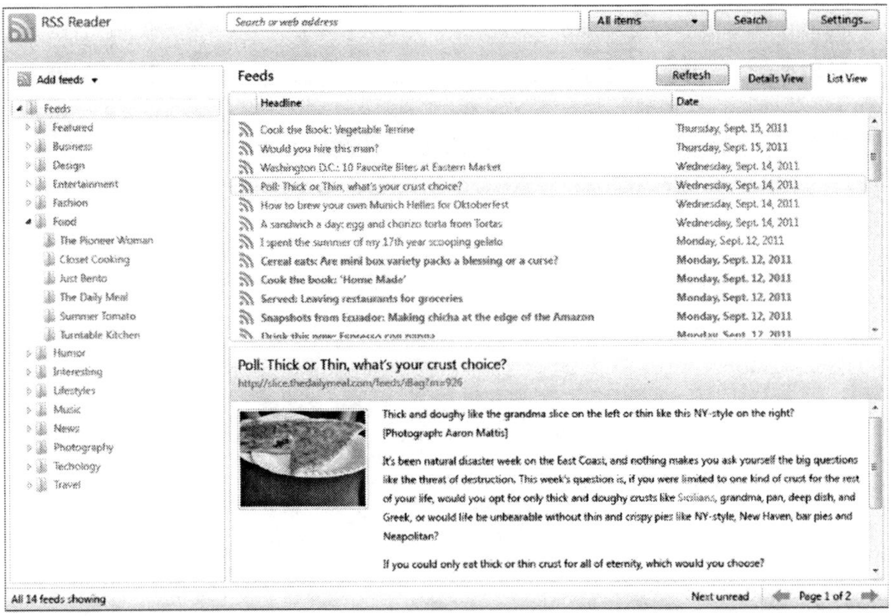

Figure 6-1. RSS Reader application we will "update" to Windows 8

The following example is based on a presentation I have given at numerous events. It is based on an example Jensen Harris used at BUILD in 2011. It is a great example of an application that needs a lot of work to be appropriate for the Windows Store. For example, this is an application that is supposed to be "best at" letting users read articles, but the region of the application available for reading an article is roughly 30 percent of the screen!

The best way to look at this example is to break it up into its fundamental components. Then, we can look at each component individually and determine where it belongs in a Windows Store application.

Let's Break It Up

The first step in figuring out what should and should not make the cut in the transition from desktop to Windows Store is to understand exactly what the application is. Figure 6-2 shows an exploded and categorized view of the RSS Reader application.

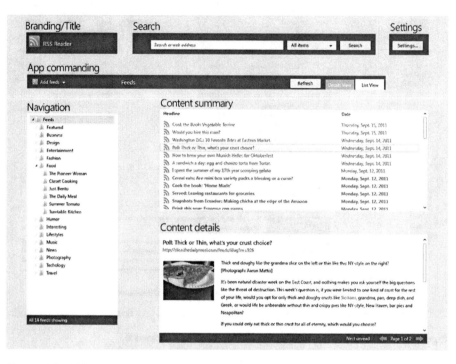

Figure 6-2. RSS Reader broken up to show the different parts of the application

Looking at the components of the application individually like this can make deciding what is essential and should be on the screen at all times and what will have to be moved off screen a much easier process. A glance at the pieces defined in Figure 6-2 reveals that there are only two sections with the word *content* in them. Given what you have learned about Windows 8 and Microsoft design, red flags should be going off in your mind. One of the major goals of this design process is to focus on the content, and we have a lot of sections here that don't deal with content that have to find a proper home. Let's take a look at each section individually and figure out what should be done with them. The goal is to review each section of the existing application against the design guidelines we have been discussing throughout this book and see how it needs to be changed to fit Windows 8.

Branding/Title

The first part of the RSS Reader we must deal with is the branding or the title. In the desktop version of the application, a logo and the title are used at the top left of the application. It should come as no surprise that we will still require logos and titles and this sort of branding in a Windows Store application. In fact, if you are using the standard type ramp and templates, the title area is even more prominent in Windows 8. There is not a whole lot to say for this section, other than to reiterate that you make sure you brand your app experience so that people will associate with your application. Figure 6-3 shows the new branding at the top of the Windows 8 application and includes the previous header for reference. The original name of the application was RSS Reader, but in the design process, we should really look to brand things better, so I've renamed the application Headlines.

Figure 6-3. Branding on Windows 8 vs. previous branding

Search

The desktop RSS Reader application has a Search bar, a drop-down to change context for the search, and a Search button at the top of the application. This is persistent in the user interface, regardless of whether the user ever performs a search. This is a perfect example of chrome that does not have to be occupying screen real estate all the time. I introduced the principle of "Do more with less" in Chapter 2, and we can use that principle here by moving our Search functionality to the Search charm in the Charms bar. The "less" part comes from the fact that Search will no longer always be on the screen. The "doing more" part refers to the fact that now, not only does the Search functionality for our app work when the user is running our application, but it will also work from anywhere in the system. This is an application of the

"Win as one" principle, because fulfilling the Search contract allows us to work together with the operating system and other applications, in order to fulfill the Search scenario for the user. Figure 6-4 shows the Search functionality and its new home on Windows 8. Note that as was covered in Chapter 4, you can add the scoping, sorting, and filtering that may be present (the dropdown in this case) to the search results page.

Figure 6-4. Search moves to the Charms bar

Settings

Settings functionality is something we discussed in Chapter 4 in detail. This RSS Reader example drives home the point about classic desktop applications having so many different ways of accessing Settings. I mentioned all of the different menu items that developers have placed "settings" under, but I did not mention that some applications have a "Settings" button right on the app's main surface. If the application has suitable default settings, the user might not ever need to click that button. This is another case where we need to leverage "Do more with less" and "Win as one" to get this persistent UI element off the screen. The bonus for doing this is that users will know exactly what to expect when they tap on Settings in the Charms bar for your app. It will be the same experience they've had everywhere else in the system. Figure 6-5 shows where the Settings functionality will move in the new design.

Figure 6-5. Settings moves to the Charms bar

App Commanding

Another section of the RSS Reader that is taking up permanent space in the interface is what I would consider the "app commanding." In the case of the RSS Reader, this consists of a button to add a feed, a "Refresh" button, and a set of tabs for list view vs. detail view. In other desktop applications, there could be a whole toolbar of such buttons. In cases requiring a large number of buttons, you will first want to pare down the list until you are left with only the essential ones. You can use the strategies we discussed in Chapter 4 in this process. The Microsoft Design Style Principles involved in this phase are "Do more with less," in that we are moving things off screen, and "Be fast and fluid," in that we are putting commands where the user will expect them. In the case of the RSS Reader application, we already have a reasonably short list, so we can keep all of them. However, instead of them always being on the screen, we will move them to the app bar. Following the rules regarding "add/create/new" buttons, we'll place the "Add feed" button on the far right of the app bar. Next to it, we can place the "Refresh" button. To balance the bar, we can put the view-related buttons on the left-hand side of the bar. Figure 6-6 shows the end result of moving the commands to the app bar.

App commanding

List view   Details view   Refresh   Add feed

Figure 6-6. Moving the commands to the app bar

Navigation

The navigation tree on the left-hand side of the RSS Reader application is the type of chrome that Windows 8 really tries to reduce reliance on. Complex hierarchical navigation trees like this are difficult to work with and manage on touch, and the Windows 8 navigation schemes have been devised to avoid them. Instead of having deep hierarchies such as this, you should aim to flatten out the hierarchy as much as possible. In this case, we are referring to a list of RSS feeds. Rather than have a nested tree the user must navigate through, aim for a flat list of categorized feeds. When using a GridView/ListView, the section headers can correspond to the individual feeds, and if you still want to have the categories, you can explore using the navigation bar at the top of the screen for this purpose. As long as you provide a good Semantic Zoom experience, as discussed in Chapter 4, users will be able to easily explore the items in your application, even if the items they are interested in are in the very last feed. We can get rid of this tree completely, as long as we make changes to integrate its functionality into our content directly. For this application, the GridView will have section headers that correspond to the feed names. Tapping one of these feed names will reveal all of the articles for that feed. This would be equivalent to selecting it in the original hierarchical tree.

Content

After we have gone through the process of moving all of the previous items off screen into their new home on Windows 8, we are left with only two sections, shown in Figure 6-7.

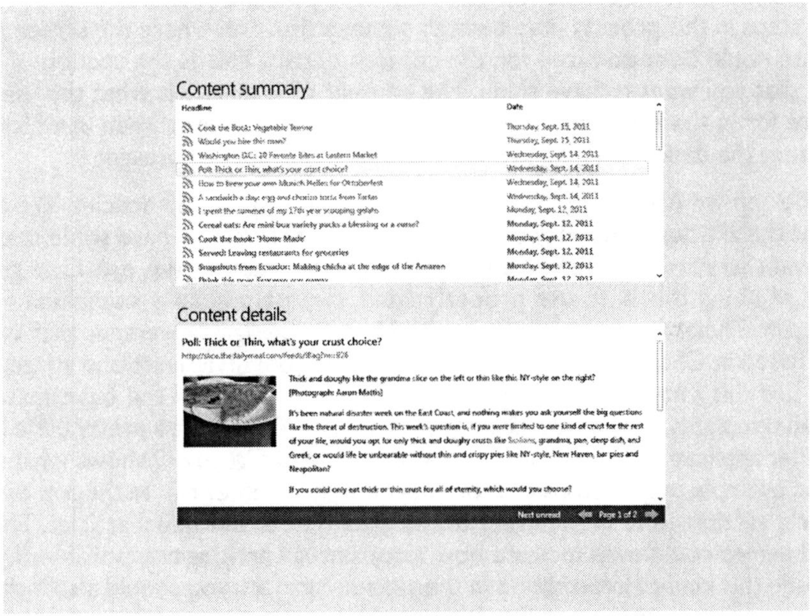

Figure 6-7. Content summary and content details

It should not come as too much of a surprise that the two areas of the application that we have not moved off screen both have the word *content* in them. After all, the mantra we have subscribed to here is "content before chrome," so once most of the chrome is gone, all we have left is content. There is still work to be done at this point, however. It would be fairly easy to stop here and say "I made it; it's all content now!" and figure out how to format what remains into something that looks like a Windows 8 app. Doing that would be missing an important step of the process, though.

Once you have reduced the application to the content, you need to take a step back and make sure you have the right content for the tasks in the app. For example, you must decide whether the content summary is important information to have constantly on the screen or not. There are definitely scenarios whereby it might be valuable to have the content summary available in list form. The most immediate example of where the content summary is almost as valuable as the content details themselves that I can think of is the e-mail summary list in an e-mail app. How many times have you opened your e-mail application just to scan the list of new e-mails? It is a very common-use case for e-mail, so it is very important in a mail application to keep the content summary on the surface at all times. Another example might be a playlist in a music application.

Whether you decide the content summary is important for your application or not, the content details will definitely be important. In fact, all of the previous steps in this process have been to set up a situation where the screen real estate could be maximized for the content details. This is the section of the app that you want to have shine. The content of your app is what the user is there for in the first place! You have just about the entire screen in which to present the data. Now you just have to figure out how to present it.

In the app we have been looking at, we want to display RSS articles. We also want the articles to be easy to preview and for the user to have some reason to want to read them. We need something that catches the eye. One great way of doing this is to use properly sized, clean typography combined with imagery. These are concepts from the Modern Design Movement that were discussed in Chapter 1. Since most RSS articles contain at least one image, we can use this image to represent the article. Taking one of the basic master-detail templates, such as the Grid Application, we can create a pretty basic RSS Reader application that would fit in on Windows 8. Figure 6-8 shows what this basic example might look like. Note how the feed names run at the top of the article sections, and the imagery draws attention to individual articles. These feed names could even indicate how many unread articles are available. If you include this kind of information in the section headers, you should also include it in your Semantic Zoom view (if applicable).

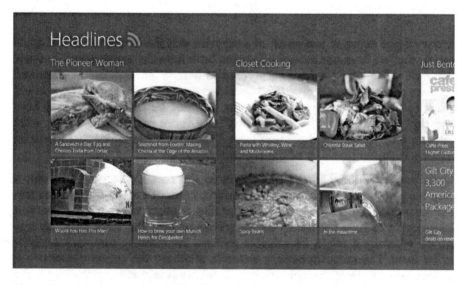

Figure 6-8. A basic conversion of the RSS Reader into a Windows 8 app

Making Your App Stand Out

The basic approach might be sufficient for your app. It is certainly acceptable at this point. The app has undergone the entire process of editing until only the content remains. We have taken the time to make sure we laid the content out according to the Windows 8 design guidelines and placed any non-content off screen in a suitable location. However, the very best applications on the platform will be the ones that push the envelope and provide an exceptional experience. In the case of news articles, one can argue that the application we should look to for inspiration is the Bing News application. There is a reason I have been using this application for many of the examples in this book. This app was designed to be a "best in breed" news application to help people understand what is possible on the Windows 8 platform. Because there are a lot of similarities between the News app and our RSS Reader, we can learn from the techniques this app used to take things to the next level. Look again at the launch experience for the News application shown, in Figure 6-9.

Figure 6-9. Launch experience of Bing News

This is anything but your usual bunch of "colored boxes" that Windows 8 applications often get characterized as. Rather, this is a highly immersive experience that presents the news in a way that draws the reader in. Using a hero graphic to make the top story stand out is a bold acknowledgment of the platform's strength in presenting this type of material. Clean typography accentuates the wonderful use of photography throughout the application.

As the user navigates further into the hierarchy of the app, this focus on typography and photographic imagery is not lost. Figure 6-10 shows the section detail for the "U.S." section.

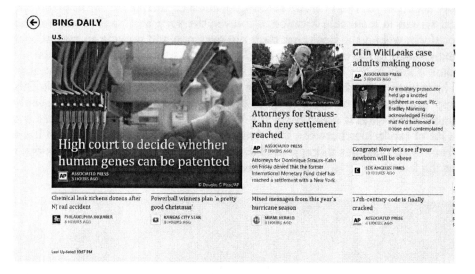

Figure 6-10. Bing News section details page still emphasizes type and images

Although at its core the Bing News application is nothing more than an aggregator of several news RSS feeds, the experience the team crafted is anything but ordinary. Careful attention to detail and proper use of Microsoft Design Style Principles leads to a first-class experience. Users will know the difference between an application that just follows the basic templates and does not attempt to do something interesting and one that tries to push the platform forward with innovative design decisions. Take the time with your application to think of ways you can enhance the experience for your users beyond the basics. A second and maybe even third pass over your initial design ideas might be the key to finding the thing that makes your application stand out. Try to find ways to highlight important information using larger grid items or imagery. Break up the monotony that comes from adhering to the standard Grid App template.

From Other Tablets to Windows 8

It is worth noting at this point that it is not enough to start from a design that has been optimized for touch and then porting it directly to Windows 8. Windows 8 is a very different platform from the iPad and other tablets that are widely in use today. Even though these platforms were designed for touch, they have different design ideals that drive the design of apps on the platform. Given the early state of the Windows Store, it's hard to find a lot of applications to compare side by side. Thankfully, Microsoft has a OneNote app on the iPad and also built a Windows Store version of OneNote from the ground up. This provides a pretty good opportunity to compare some of the major differences between these two platforms. Figure 6-11 is the iPad version of OneNote, and Figure 6-12 is the Windows Store version. Both have been opened to the same relatively empty notebook for a more even comparison. A border has been added to the Windows 8 screenshot for use on the page, but it does not exist in the app.

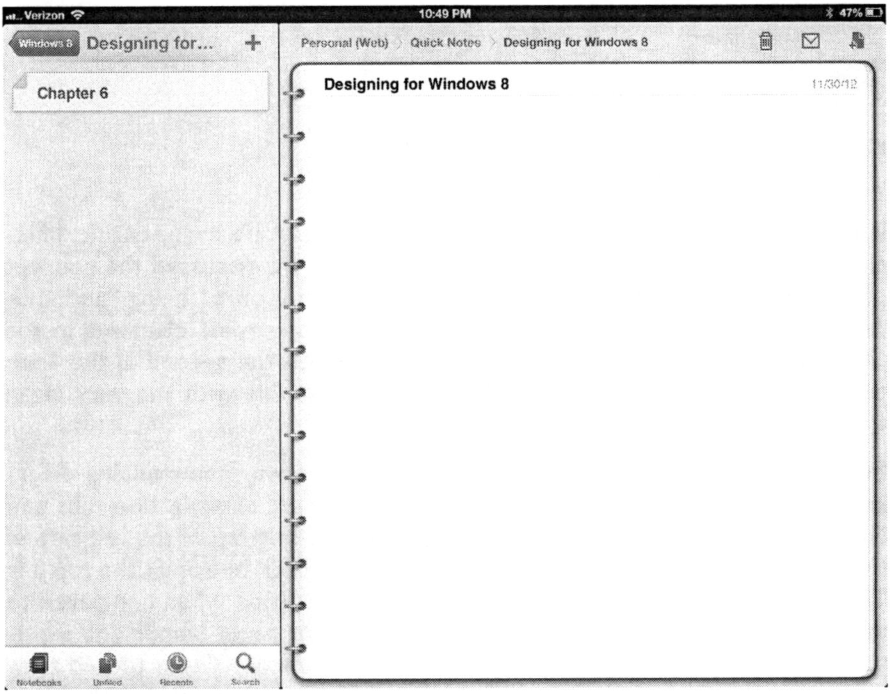

Figure 6-11. OneNote on the iPad

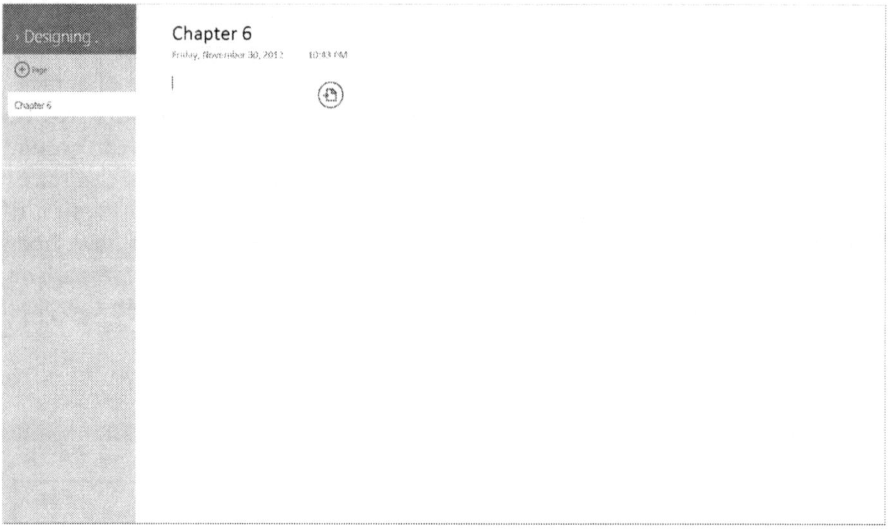

Figure 6-12. OneNote on Windows 8

It should probably be immediately apparent that there are huge stylistic differences between the two applications. In Chapter 2, we discussed the concept of skeuomorphism and how it goes against the notion of being "authentically digital." The iPad application has a few skeuomorphic elements in the OneNote design. The first is the ringed binder, and the second is the linen pattern that the notebook is resting on. Contrast this with the very clean typography-driven Windows 8 application.

Even more important than stylistic decisions is the way commanding differs in these applications. The iPad applications have a set of navigation tabs and buttons above the notebook page, a tab bar at the bottom of the left side of the screen that includes Search functionality, and a back button at the top left. That is a lot of chrome on the surface of the application when compared to the Windows 8 UI. The Windows 8 app has a "New page" button and a button to launch a contextual radial menu. All other functionality is tucked away in the app bar, Charms bar, or only appears when needed (true task-driven design in action!). This makes it much easier to focus on the notes the user is trying to capture in OneNote.

Speaking of that radial menu button, the radial menu in the Windows Store version of OneNote is one of the more innovative features I have seen in Windows 8 app design so far. At first glance, this approach seems to violate the approach of putting contextual actions in the app bar. However, with the large number of possible interactions covered by this radial menu, it is easy to see that the app bar approach would not scale in this case. The end result of trying to cram all that functionality into the app bar would be a fairly poor user experience. For one thing, there would simply be too many buttons. Also, either the app bar would have to be persistently on the screen or would constantly be popping up. For these reasons, I think it is a great idea to explore alternative commanding options, if you have an action-heavy application idea. If you have not seen the radial menu in action yet, I recommend downloading OneNote from the Windows Store and checking it out. For now, take a look at it expanded to the first level, in Figure 6-13.

Figure 6-13. OneNote's radial menu is truly innovative

As I briefly alluded, the radial menu is contextual, so it will change, depending on what you have selected. As you tap on segments of the menu, another circle of options will appear. This is a very touch-friendly way to do a menu system for a variety of things, such as font sizing, creating tables, creating lists, etc. New UI paradigms such as this will emerge as we begin to embrace the content before chrome nature of these clean, touch-driven interfaces. It is an interesting time to be a designer, with basically a blank canvas on which to create truly new ideas. Who knows, maybe in future versions of books such as this, a reader will be credited with having created something as innovative as the radial menu!

Summary

In this chapter, I tied together many of the concepts we have discussed in this book. First, I walked through an example of transferring a classic desktop application over to Windows 8 as a Windows Store application. Along the way, I reviewed many principles from the first five chapters of the book. I then highlighted some of the differences between apps developed for the iPad and Windows Store by comparing the OneNote app on these two platforms.

At this point, you are armed with all of the basic knowledge you need to be a successful Windows 8 application designer. There are many resources provided by Microsoft and the community at large to help you expand your knowledge. My hope is that this book has provided a great launching point for that trip and that you are well on your way to realizing your first big hit in the Windows Store. If you get an app in there, be sure to let me know.

Index

A

Anatomy of a Murder, 10

App bar, 33
    button
        advantages, 80
        brainstorming scenario, 78
        group commands, 79
        icons, 83
        menu creation, 80
        placements, 80
        refinement strategy, 77
    mouse-and-keyboard setup, 77
    styling considerations, 83

B

Bauhaus design style
    Gropius, Walter, 2
    Running Total, 2

Blend ship, 36

C

Charm bar, 17

Cinematography and motion design, 10

Collaborative process, 61

D, E

Digital prototyping
    computer software, 64
    definition, 64
    strengths, 67
    tools, 68

button's click interaction, 65
    Indigo Studio, 65
    RecipeLater, 66
    run, 65
    static mockups, 64
    time line, 66
    weakness, 67

Direct manipulation, 115

F, G

Form factor and layout
    fill view, 125
    landscape vs. portrait
        iBing News article, 120
        landscape first, 117
        orientation, 119
        1366x768 resolution, 117
        Tweetro, 121
        Windows 8 Start screen, 118
    screen densities
        bitmaps, 129
        scale percentage, 129
        typographic grid units, 130
        vector graphics, 129
    screen sizes
        adaptive layout, larger screens, 127
        fixed layout, large screens, 126
    snapped view design, 123

H

Hub page
    advantage, 48
    content analysis, 53

Hub page (*cont.*)
    Grid Application template, 49
    hierarchic structural information, 50
    item details page, 52
    News application, 49–50
    planning strategy, 52
    Running Total application, 53
    section details page, 50–51
    Semantic Zoom, 53
    specific article, 51–52
    Start screen, 48
    U.S. news section, 50–51

I, J, K

International typographic style
    bold color, 10
    iconography, 7–8
    photographic imagery, 8
    typographic grids, 4–5
    typography, 6

L

Live Tile, 11

M

Microsoft design language, 134
Microsoft design style principles, 144
    authentically digital
        bold colors, 27
        cloud connectedness, 28
        skeuomorphism, 24, 26
        typography, 27
    be fast and fluid
        animation/motion design, 22–23
        application responsiveness and
            readiness, 23
        designing for touch, 20
    craftsmanship pride
        align to Windows 8 design grid, 18
        definition, 14
        platform consistency, 15
        safe and reliable application, 16
    do more with less
        be great at something, 29
        content before chrome, 30, 32
        inspire confidence, 33

win as one
    fit into UI model, 35
    tools and templates usage, 36
    work together, 35
Microsoft's guiding principles, 112

N

Navigation bar
    Bing applications, 58
    content switching, 58
    edge gesture, 56
    flat hierarchy, 59
    HealthGraph API, 59
    Internet Explorer, 56
    Running Total, 59
    viewing modes, 57
    visual fashion, 57
North by Northwest, 10

O

Outlook *vs.* Windows 8 Mail, 31

P, Q

Persistent commands, 81
Psycho, 10

R

RunKeeper, 30

S

Screen—map and chart, 21
Search charm
    content search, 85
    results
        display, 90
        ordering, 89
        Windows store, 89
    Search pane
        installed applications, 85
        query suggestions, 86
        result suggestion, 88
        Semantic Zoom, 111
    XAML/HTML, 92
"Search map" button, 82

Semantic Zoom, 111

Settings flyout, 17

Share charm
information sharing, 93
QuickLink, 96
recipe application, 93
Settings charm, 97
Settings flyout
creation, WinJS, 99
creation, XAML, 100
design, 98
Settings pane, 97–98
Share flyout, 94–95
Share Target, 93–94

Share Source contract, 84

Share Target contract, 84

Skeuomorphism, 24

Standard Grid App template, 144

Swiss design style. *See* International
typographic style

T, U

Touch design
desktop mode, 109
direct manipulation, 115
mouse pointer, 115
move onscreen elements, 115
pressed down item, 116
task-centered design, 116
touch language
App commands, 113
pinch and stretch to
zoom, 111
press and hold gesture, 111
Semantic Zoom, 111
swipe to select, 111, 113
system commands, 113
tablet/touchscreen
phone, 111
touch targets, 114

Tweetro application, 76

Tweetro's main interface, 95

V

Vertigo, 10

Visual Studio, 36

W, X, Y, Z

Windows 8 app
"best at" statement
definition, 40
differentiation, 41
real-world, 42
Running Total, 42, 46
specificity, 40
bottom edge (*see* App bar)
brainstorming scenario
objective, 44
Running Total, 44
Charms bar
contracts concept, 84
flyout, 84
Search charm (*see* Search charm)
Share charm (*see* Share charm)
system-driven functionality, 83
crossed-out features, 45
GridView
horizontal grid format, 72
layout exploration, 76
main hub, 72
template, colorful imagery, 73
template, gray boxes, 72
tile size variation, 75
TopFlix, 74
navigation and content strategy
bar (*see* Navigation bar)
browsability, 48
hub (*see* Hub page)
screen real estate, 47
prototyping
digital (*see* Digital prototyping)
importance, 60
paper prototyping, 62
sketching, 60, 62
visual design mock-ups, 68
removing scenario, 45–46
Semantic Zoom
Bing News application, 107
discoverability, 103
fundamental design, 103
Running Total, 107
WinJS implementation, 105
XAML implementation, 106
tablets
apps design, 144
iPad application, 145

Windows 8 app (*cont.*)
    New UI paradigms, 147
    radial menu, 146
UI patterns, 133
Windows desktop applications
    app commanding, 139
    Bing News application, 143–144
    branding/title, 136
    classic applications, 134
    clean typography, 143
    components, 135
    content details, 142
    content summary, 141
    e-mail app, 141
    launch experience, 143
    Microsoft design language, 134

    navigation, 140
    RSS articles, 142
    RSS Reader, 134, 142
    Search bar, 137
    Settings, 138
    standard Grid App template, 144
    touch target size, 134
Windows 8 design style. See Bauhaus design
        style; International typographic
        style; Cinematography and
        motion design
Windows 8 platform
    form factor and layout (see Form factor
        and layout)
    snapped view design, 123
    touch design (see Touch design)

CPSIA information can be obtained at www.ICGtesting.com
Printed in the USA
LVOW070712020313

322388LV00010B/468/P